1701 9100 318 600 1

WITHDRAWN
Salina Public Library

Easy Peasy Potty Training

The Busy Parents' Guide to Toilet Training
with Less Stress and Less Mess

Julie Schooler

Copyright © 2015 Julie Schooler

All rights reserved. No part of this publication may be reproduced, distributed, or transmitted in any form or by any means, including photocopying, recording, or other electronic or mechanical methods, without the prior written permission of the publisher, except in the case of brief quotations embodied in reviews and certain other non-commercial uses permitted by copyright law.

Salina Public Library
Salina, Kansas
YOUTH SERVICES DEPT,

DISCLAIMER

This toilet training guide is designed to give parents and caregivers some useful tips and ideas. It does not replace expert advice from medical or behavioral specialists. It is recommended that you seek advice from qualified practitioners if you are concerned in any way.

This book is dedicated to my son Dylan,
a beautiful tiny human.
I love you to the moon and back.

DOWNLOAD THE
BUSY PARENT SUMMARY

For all you wonderful, busy parents, I have created a summary sheet of the main actions to take and shopping items to buy for toilet training.

Head to cherishmama.com and get hold of your copy today.

Contents

I Can't Believe I Am Reading A Book About Potty Training

The Dark Side

Welcome to the world of potty training. This is the dark side of parenting - dirty, difficult and a little bit dangerous.

It's not something you want to go through and certainly not something you want to read about. However, you realize you need to do something about it.

- Do you want your child to be toilet trained easily and quickly but have no clue where to start and are worried that it could all go wrong?
- Or have you started potty training your toddler and it's all turned to custard so you desperately need some solutions?

Then you have come to the right place.

This book is a simple to follow, step-by-step process to toilet train your child. It answers all of your burning questions, busts myths and misconceptions and tells you what to do if there are mishaps, problems or hiccups. All the tools and techniques you will ever need for toilet training are right here.

You won't need to spend hours searching for information all over the Internet. You will have a clear direction and won't be confused by conflicting advice. There is no need to repeat mistakes made by other parents.

This book has everything you need to know about toilet training and nothing you don't. It will save you time, money and your sanity during this challenging stage.

One book. Potty training. Done.

Why this Book was Written

I have potty trained exactly one child so far, my son Dylan. I read a lot of books and articles, searched all over the Internet and even took a course on potty training.

But there was a gap. Yes, there are lots of books out there. But, surprisingly, I could not find one, relatively short, clear, gimmick-free guide to potty training. This is the book I wish I had when I was potty training Dylan.

I surveyed dozens of other parents who have toilet trained their children. The research I undertook plus all their answers have been combined into a simple blueprint to toilet train your child. You not only get to avoid all the mistakes we have made, but will have answers on hand for any issues that arise. Their stories and tips are scattered throughout the book.

In this book there is no pressure to 'potty train in three days' or 'get out of diapers in a day'. There are no strange orders to throw out all your unused diapers, put a gate across your bathroom door or limit your child's liquid intake. In here are plain instructions that help you tackle the challenge of potty training your little one.

The Benefits

I don't need to tell you how great it is when your little one is out of diapers and fully toilet trained, but here is just a small assortment of benefits:

- As a parent – you can pat yourself on the back as you just assisted your child to achieve a major developmental milestone.
- For your child – He has learnt a really important skill that takes him another step towards his independence, plus he has pride in his capabilities.
- For both of you – there is a stronger bond from getting to know your child even better and assisting her to learn a vital life skill.
- Environmental – no more disposable diapers being sent to landfill.
- Time – more time to spend with your family doing fun things and not changing diapers.
- Money – more cold hard cash available as you are not spending it all on diapers.

My Promise to You

If you follow the simple step-by-step process in this book, your toddler will be out of diapers and fully toilet trained in a quick, easy and stress-free way.

If you start toilet training and it goes wrong, then it's not too late.

The comprehensive problems and solutions section literally helps you clean up the mess. Your little boy is afraid to flush the toilet? Your little girl loves to flush the toilet repeatedly? The solutions to these common problems, and many more, are all in this book.

What Have You Got to Lose?

Let's face it, how much do you really want to read on this subject? All you need to know has been chunked down into a few easily digestible chapters.

Don't be wondering whether you should let your boy pee standing up, what to do at swimming lessons, or whether you need a travel potty. Get the answers to these uncertainties and more in this book.

Start reading this book today and start potty training tomorrow – the right way, once, first time.

When You Should Not Read this Book

This book is for parents and caregivers of toddlers over 18 months. It does not include strategies to get your baby out of diapers before this age. This is called 'elimination communication,' and even the name sounds nasty and hard. There are plenty of other books that explain how to do it if you want to go down that bumpy road.

Note also that this book does not specifically address toilet training for children with developmental delays, intellectual issues or medical problems. Nor does it directly provide advice for parents of twins and triplets. The general advice in this book will certainly help, but there are other books and resources that tackle the extra considerations for these situations.

We Are All Adults Here

By now I think you have realized that if you want a dry, long-winded, textbook that has every last detail about toilet training, you have come to the wrong place. There is no history of toilet training here, very few definitions (if you are here you already know what a potty is), and the science is kept to a minimum. You have probably already taught your child the best way to wash and dry his hands. You don't need a book for that.

You are a busy parent and I am not here to waste your time. Each chapter is purposely short and easily digestible. It's best to read the book from the beginning, but if you are a 'meat and potatoes' kind of person, then just skip to the 'how to' chapters. If you have a tendency to worry about what can go wrong, then don't read the problems and solutions section unless you are faced with a particular issue.

This book guides you, but also treats you like an adult. You will have to make some decisions, and almost certainly there will be mistakes, but hopefully you can have a bit of a laugh along the way.

Now Let's Please Have Some Fun

Yes, you are learning this stuff only as a means to help your child gain a new and important skill of how to go to the toilet, but this does not exclude humor from entering the equation. After all, if you can't have a bit of a laugh during a time when there is talk of toilets, potties, bottoms, pee and poop, then it is a sad life indeed. So kick back, pour yourself a wine, and delve into the world of toilet training.

ACTION ITEM - Buy a little notebook.

Then get ready to record some absolute gems because your toddler is guaranteed to come out with them.

Daddy Story – I took my little girl to the toilet just before bed. She peed and I asked her if there was anything more to come. She replied, "No, the poo is sleeping". - Marcus

CHAPTER TWO

Toilet Talk

Potty Training Versus Toilet Training

You would not be interested in this topic if you didn't have a vague idea about what it entails. However, just so we are all on the same page, the Merriam-Webster dictionary definition of toilet training is:

"The process of training a (young) child to understand and control their bladder and bowel movements and to use the toilet".

It is mostly accepted that for general use, 'potty training' is the same as 'toilet training'. So whether you decide to train your child with a potty or a toilet or both (much more on this later), the process is referred to as potty training or toilet training interchangeably throughout the book.

Your Tiny Human

This book is for parents and caregivers of children between 18 months and four years old. Your child will be addressed in a number of different ways including:

- child
- young child
- toddler

- little one
- young one
- tot
- tiny human

It also means that sometimes I refer to your child as 'he' and sometimes as 'she'. The use of he or she has been alternated throughout the book. If a section, story or paragraph refers to 'he' and your child is a 'she,' then change the pronoun in your head (and vice versa).

No Need for Potty Mouth

Due to the nature of the book, many words that may not be considered part of polite conversation come up often. If you want a book that sticks to proper scientific names such as 'stool,' 'feces' or 'urination,' you have come to the wrong place. Your child is not a lab rat. She is a tiny human who has normal bodily functions.

I mainly use what is considered acceptable slang or informal language with a scattering of some proper words. Most words are considered okay to say in front of Nana. That is (and I dare you to get through this list without at least a bit of a smile):

- Bathroom – toilet, loo, lavatory, restroom, commode
- Body parts (front) – privates, penis, vagina
- Body parts (back) – backside, bottom, bum, bum-bum, tush, rear
- Urine – pee-pee, pee, going for a tinkle, number ones or (occasionally if I am feeling posh) emptying the bladder
- Feces – poo, poop, number twos, or (occasionally if I am feeling posh) bowel movements

- Flatulence – passing gas, breaking wind, fluff, fart, pop-pop
- Underwear – underpants, undies, knickers, briefs
- Having no underwear on – going commando, nudies

ACTION ITEM – Decide on your 'toilet talk'.
This is your chance to get thinking (if you haven't already) about what you want to call these bodily functions, toileting words and anatomical areas in your family.

Grab any other significant adults in your household and have a talk about what words you would be comfortable using in and out of the house. You may want to do this on your first glass of wine, but it's not recommended you wait to your third. Don't spend ages on this. Have a giggle and then move on.

CHAPTER THREE
Don't Worry, Be Happy

Worry Lines

It's not surprising that the thought of potty training stresses most parents out. It is a topic that:

- you probably know very little about, and
- what you do know sounds difficult, messy and full of conflicting messages.

It is a strange place to be – to lack knowledge and simultaneously feel overwhelmed, but that sums up potty training in a nutshell.

Destination Disaster

All your worries end at the same destination – the potential for potty training to turn into a disaster. Common worries include:

- I don't know what I am doing.
- Potty training could take a lot of time and effort.
- All that time and effort and it may not even work.
- I will start toilet training too early and my tot won't get it.
- I will leave it too late and my child will be so used to wearing diapers that she won't want to get out of them.
- How do I make sure my child learns everything without being too tough on him?
- It has the potential to ruin my carpet.

- My child will never ever learn to go to the toilet properly and will end up wearing diapers at high school.

Okay, maybe that last one doesn't reflect every parent's concerns, but you are probably nodding your head at some of the items on the worry list.

Why You Don't Need to Worry So Much
There are three reasons why you don't need to worry so much.

First, big kudos to you as you have picked up or downloaded this book. Just doing so makes you an A1 amazing parent. You are getting the strategies to help you through the toilet training process. You will get answers to your questions and solutions to problems. It is all in here. Drop those shoulders. Relax.

Second, people love to fill your head with the bad stories - repeated bed-wetting, carpet cleaning costs or a discovery of poop wall art. At the end of the day, no two potty training journeys are exactly the same, so don't worry about what you have heard already.

Last, you have probably realized by now that whatever you are worried about most will almost certainly not be the thing that trips you up. It will be something that blindsides you completely. The universe is funny that way. Well perhaps this may not comfort you at all but it is just a fact. We spent many months with a toddler who was 100% toilet trained for pee but refused to poop in the potty. I had absolutely no idea that this is a common problem. How this got resolved is discussed later (warning - it may be considered a bit controversial).

ACTION ITEM – Ignore Everyone

If people want to tell you their 'horror' potty training stories, ask them not to, or if you can't do that, then listen to it and then remove it from your head immediately. Do whatever it takes to keep your shoulders lowered and the worry lines away.

CHAPTER FOUR

Two Main Myths

Busting Myths

The two predominant myths surrounding toilet training children actually conflict with each other. Busting through both of these gets to the heart of what worries us as parents so much. Not just with potty training, but with everything we do as parents.

The Myth of the Child who Potty Trains Herself

No child in the history of the world has ever toilet trained herself. This myth rears its ugly head when other people say things like, "My child toilet trained in a couple of days, no accidents and she was done." You are hoping against hope that this will be your child, but I am telling you right now that it won't be.

Think about it - no child has ever woken up one day and thought, "I am over this comfortable diaper thing where my mommy does everything for me. I will now put these flimsy, thin underpants on and find a small, dark room with a big scary white thing in it. I will then do my business into a cavernous hole that makes my pee and poo disappear with a loud sound."

Peeing and pooping are natural bodily functions. Recognizing that you are about to pee and poop and finding an appropriate place in which to do these things requires learning new things. You, as the parent, need to assist that learning.

The trouble with this myth is that parents who even sort of believe it leave the potty training up to the child. Of course, they do some of the work, but they don't jump in the deep end and commit to a focused, positive attempt at toilet training. Then when they hit the first hurdle, their child is back in diapers and Mom and Dad are wondering what went wrong.

The Myth that Potty Training is Seriously Hard Work

On the flipside, many parents are concerned about pouring their time, energy and resources into something that could take a long time, ruin the carpet and may not even work. This myth originates in the 'potty training horror stories' we are told. There is a worry that even with a focused attempt, the child will not master this new skill, or worse, rebel against the idea entirely.

The trouble with this myth is that it implies that potty training has to be a significant effort only on the part of the parent. It excludes the child from the equation, even though he is front and center of it. Parents who believe this can get caught up in overly complicating potty training by adding in bells and whistles that are not needed (a flushing, music-playing potty, complete with own toilet paper holder anyone?) Or they give themselves unnatural deadlines that stress everyone out.

What Potty Training is Really About

Potty training is a major test of parenting skills and only works when there is a good combination of the child and the parent. This means really trying to understand your child, including his learning style, developmental stage and temperament. It also means understanding yourself, including your approach to teaching, as well as how much time, energy and focus you are willing to invest in assisting your child on her journey to gain this vital life skill.

Toilet training is not something outside of parenting that needs to be over and done with. Try to see this as a good opportunity to sharpen all those parenting skills that will be needed even more as your child grows.

Take a deep breath. Potty training is pulling out all the positivity, patience, consistency and ability to repeat yourself without getting annoyed that you can muster. It is also being able to deal with bodily functions and accidents in a calm, neutral and respectful way.

You Will Succeed

Please know that your child <u>will</u> be toilet trained. It may take longer than you expect, there may be hiccups along the way, but it <u>will</u> happen.

This book is a step-by-step guide to potty training with solutions to common problems. It assists you to toilet train your child. However -

1. You know your child and your family situation. I do not. This guide holds your hand, but if you don't like some of the advice, solutions or processes in here, then just don't follow them.

2. You need to make some decisions along the way. This guide spells out the decisions, but ultimately you need to make them.

3. Know that if you decide on something and it doesn't work you can change it. Don't start anything you can't change, but know that you can change anything! Tweaking to make something work better is a rational choice, not an acceptance of failure.

The bad news is that there is no magic blue pill for potty training. You have to suck it up and do the work. You have some decisions to make. Some things will go wrong. Be okay with that. The good news is that the process in this book is guaranteed to work because you determine the best way to toilet train for your circumstances.

Now we have busted potty training myths, let's answer some of your burning questions.

CHAPTER FIVE

Three Main Questions

Question One – How Long Does Potty Training Take and What Does Being Fully Trained Look Like?

There is no one-size-fits-all answer to how long potty training takes. Per the definition stated earlier, there are two main parts to toilet training. First, the child needs to understand her bladder and bowel signals. She needs to go from having no clue to knowing that she peed/pooped, to realizing she is currently peeing/pooping and then finally that she needs to pee/poop.

The second, and equally as crucial part, is when he realizes he is about to pee or poop, he knows to go to a potty or toilet to do his business.

The first part can take between a couple of days and a couple of weeks usually. In order to facilitate this, this book advocates a method of a few days of extremely dedicated focus (the short intense stage). To cement the learning on the second part, there is a Stage Two of active maintenance. See later chapters for all the details on these. By the end of these two stages, a child should have progressed to the point that she recognizes signals and can get to the toilet most of the time, with or without your help.

After that, all going well, toileting your toddler fades into the fabric of everyday life. Your toddler will go off to the potty or toilet on his own more and more. Sometimes you won't even know he has gone. There may be the occasional accident, but when a child learns to ride a bike, he sometimes falls off, too.

In short, and I am sorry to be the one to break it to you, but most people are looking at three to six months for a child to be reliably dry, with only the rare accident, and mostly self-initiate going to the toilet.

Note, and this is a big note - this excludes being toilet trained at night, which is quite different again. See the "Nighttime" chapter for more details.

Question Two – Should I Train for Pee and Poo at the Same Time?

In a word – Yes. This is an example in which parents can overthink things and make them more complicated than they are. Yes, she will pee more in proportion to poop, and yes, the brain and body signals are different, but it is too confusing to separate them out. I am not even sure how you would. Sometimes it is harder to coax the poo, but that shouldn't stop you from trying to toilet train for number ones and twos together.

Question Three – Is There a Difference Between Girls and Boys?

Of course there are anatomical differences between girls and boys, but how you potty train them is pretty much the same, at least at first. Some research seems to indicate that girls can show signs of readiness earlier and so can be trained slightly earlier than boys, but forget about statistics and just concentrate on your child as he or she is.

For the first couple of months, while you are in the active phases, both girls and boys should sit down on the toilet or potty (with a boy tucking his penis down to pee). This helps both genders relax and feel comfortable in the new environment and has the added bonus that if he poops at the same time, it is contained.

So when do boys stand to pee? Most people find this happens naturally over time. Usually he sees Daddy or an older brother pee that way and wants to model their behavior. If it doesn't happen organically, show him when he is tall enough to stand so he is not touching the toilet seat and has the dexterity to balance himself properly.

When boys start standing up there are two main things to learn. First, they need to aim properly. There are all sorts of things that can be placed in the toilet to encourage aiming (special stickers, corks, ping pong balls) so feel free to go down this track if you think it will help. Otherwise, your little man should just get better over time. Teach him from a young age to use some toilet paper or a wipe to clean up any spilled drops and you will be bringing up a man that will be invited back to places.

Second, he needs to learn when and where it is appropriate to stand and pee. Outside in your private backyard is usually okay, but in the middle of picnic area at a popular children's playground is probably not. Just because he has the anatomical ability to pee anywhere, anytime, does not give him the right to do so. In fact, in some places he can get arrested for it, so it's important to teach him to be discreet.

Mama Tip — Buy a lemon tree. Peeing on a lemon tree produces a great bounty of this sour yellow fruit. Your little man will LOVE practicing 'peeing like Daddy', even if you are not the biggest fan of this practice. - Jade

CHAPTER SIX
Goals

Set Some Goals

Before you start for real, you must set some goals. Some goals, you say? Some goals for potty training? Really?

Yes really. Now hear me out.

To help you define your goals, I want you answer these few simple questions. This will bring some of those wispy wishes you have in the back of your mind to the forefront, knock back any worries and give you a clear direction for potty training.

1) When do you want your child to be toilet trained?

If your answer is within three days, then you have picked up the wrong book. Go and get one of the 47 other books that promise this.

If your answer is by a certain age, or by a certain point in time, or in a realistic period of time, then you are in the right place. For example, you want her toilet trained by her third birthday in two months' time. That is a lovely goal. Tick.

If you are still not sure what you want, then bring up what you don't want. Do you want her to be in diapers at high school? What about the first day of primary school? No, and no? Well work backwards from there.

2) How do you want the process to go?

Not sure? Well do you want it to be a battle, stressful, hard work? No, of course not. Do you want the process to be simple, effective and easy? Do you want to feel calm and positive? Do you want to minimize issues or at least have effective strategies to deal with any that arise? Put those intentions to the front.

3) What do you want your child to learn?

You want him to understand bodily functions and going to the toilet as normal things. You want him to have appropriate and acceptable language for body parts and the toileting process. And you want him to learn all this without getting scared, upset, nervous or anxious.

Keep Your Eye on the Prize

The end goal here is another step in your child becoming independent. Know that with each major milestone like this comes some frustration, but ultimately it is worth it.

ACTION ITEM – Set Some Goals
Create a list that is similar to this:

- She is out of daytime diapers by x time / in x amount of time,
- using a simple, effective and focused method,
- and a calm and positive approach,

- with minimal problems and with ability to deal with any issues,
- so that she sees going to the toilet as another normal part of daily life.

CHAPTER SEVEN

When To Start?

When Do We Start?

If you have bought this book, then you most likely want to start sooner rather than later, and you may have already seen some signs that your child wants to toilet train. However, external factors, your child's development and your own readiness must all weigh in to determine when to start.

External Factor Number One – Pick a Good Time of the Year

Toilet training preferably happens in the warmer months. This means your child can –

1. Wear fewer clothes (or none at all)
2. Be outside more

Pack away those overalls, and remove any belts or finicky-buttoned clothing for now. Anything with an elastic waistband is best. You can even encourage him to wear no pants or no clothes at all.

Some say that going commando is an essential part of the process, and others say it's a complete no-no. Your child may embrace the nude option (and you find it impossible to get him to wear clothes ever again), or he may really want to wear pants of some sort. This is a joint decision for both of you to make.

Being outside means accidents don't happen in the house (and therefore on the floor) and so become even less of a big deal, especially if your child has no pants on.

Mama Story - A lot of potty training a boy is being naked and running around the yard (at least that's how it went for us). One day my little son came running inside and all aghast, said, "The dog ate my poo poo!" I said, "Wait, you pooped in the yard?" and my son answered, "Yeah! And the dog ate it!" I didn't know whether to laugh or feel sick. - Joan

External Factor Number Two – Pick a Time with the Least Change

If possible, try to schedule the initial stage of toilet training for a time when there are no major upheavals and distractions. This means if there is a new baby, a house move or a vacation planned, you should delay starting. And do not even contemplate starting if anyone is sick.

I know this is easier said than done. For example, many of you may be expecting another child and want to get toilet training 'out of the way' before new baby arrives. Just the fact that mommy has a baby in her tummy may be too much change for your toddler, let alone learning a new complex skill. But for other children it may not be a big deal and potty training works fine. You know your child's ability for learning new information and dealing with changes, so use that knowledge in your decision of when to start.

Is Your Child Ready?

Your child's readiness to potty train has nothing to do with whether you are ready and is certainly not related to being a so-called 'good parent'. Like learning to walk, being able to go to the toilet is a developmental milestone that occurs at different times with different children. You are just there to assist with the trickier aspects of it.

Whether your child is ready is only mildly related to her age. Sure, at under a year old, most children are almost always too young. Let's say you want her toilet trained by her first day of school. Between her first and fifth birthday is a very large age range.

Being ready to be toilet trained is more about brain development and physical dexterity. His grey matter has to grow all those neurons and synapses to be able to recognize the need to empty his bladder or do a bowel movement. This is a very difficult concept to explain, and he just has to 'get it'. Part of toilet training is helping to strengthen all those connections.

She must also have the physical ability to walk (or run) to the bathroom to do her business. The other part of toilet training is teaching her to get to the potty on time.

In short, between 18 months and three years old is a good age to begin this transition. Any younger and the connections may not be there; any older and the habit of wearing a diaper could be more difficult to break.

Signs of Readiness in Your Child

"Mama, I want to be out of my diapers now, I want to be a big girl and wear underpants," said no child ever.

So how do you know if your child is ready? Luckily there are some clearly established signs of readiness.

<u>Physical Signs of Readiness</u>

- Can he move around by himself?
- Would she be able to pull her pants up and down?
- Does he sometimes remove his diaper by himself?
- Does she have regular bowel movements?
- Is his diaper dry for longer periods, say two hours or more? (check after a daytime nap)
- Can she recognize that she is going pee or poop – for example, does she go behind the couch to do a bowel movement?
- Advanced sign: Can he recognize the need to go or even control it (eg: in the bath)?

<u>Mental Signs of Readiness</u>

- Can he understand simple instructions such as 'go and get teddy'?
- Does your delightful child talk about pee and poo (usually when Grandma is visiting)?
- Can she understand the difference between wet and dry?
- Does he look like he feels uncomfortable in a wet or dirty diaper (does he pull at it)?
- Advanced sign: Does she tell you (with words or actions) that she doesn't like her wet or dirty diaper on, or that she needs to go?

Emotional or Social Signs of Readiness

- Does she display her independence ("I do it")?
- Does he like watching you and others go to the toilet (lucky you!)?
- Does she like to imitate you or others (want to wash her hands or flush the toilet)?
- Is there is a desire to please you?
- Advanced sign: Does he show an interest in going to the toilet himself?

If your child is showing none of these signs, then he is not ready. Do NOT start toilet training. But don't wait for every single one to occur. Just decide if he has shown enough of these to give it a go.

Mama Story – Evie took violently against her cloth diaper and one day just ripped it off and waved it around her head. The contents flicked over her, the room and me. That is how I knew Evie was ready to start using the toilet - she could have just told me. - Terri

Are You Ready?

Just because your child is ready does not mean that you are. A lot of people do not like to admit how hard it can be to realize they no longer have a little baby. It's perfectly okay to give yourself time to be a bit emotional about this. Then move on - your child is growing up and that comes with a whole new bunch of joys and challenges.

First, do not listen to or give in to pressure from others. Just because your friend's daughter was potty trained by two doesn't mean your child should be. If you need them to back off but want to be nice about it, try these phrases: "We are almost at that stage, not ready yet," or "We are working on it."

Second, you need to be 100% committed. (Buying this book is a good start.) Are you determined to give this a good go, to see it through, to not give up even if there are a few hiccups? If your child is not getting the idea at all, a reset into diapers for a few more weeks may be needed (more on this later). But if you see signs of progress, then you need to commit to continuing, even if there are more accidents than you would like.

Third, during potty training you need to be all the things you are meant to be as a parent but in a super-duper, Mary Poppins kind of way. Attributes you practice every day but need even more during this time include:

- being consistent and embracing repetition – this is how they learn,
- being calm and relaxed and not showing anger,
- being supportive, encouraging and patient,
- being positive and excited about going to the toilet and able to make a big deal out of it, at least for the first few days or weeks (no matter how silly you feel).

Finally, you need to develop your super-sleuth powers. Your child is unlikely to calmly state that she needs to go potty. More than likely she will 'tell' you in other ways. Look out for these signs:

- Fidgeting, jiggling, wiggling, shifting from foot to foot
- Dancing ('doing the potty/toilet/pee-pee dance')
- Crossing her legs

- Clutching at his crotch area
- Going quiet or silent
- A panicked or pleading look on her face
- More for poop – grunting, going red in the face, looking relieved or hiding in a corner or behind the couch (these may indicate you are too late.)

Your child may exhibit all or none of these, but keep your senses alert for these telltale indications of a need to go.

I Am Confused, Should I Start?

YES! All your stars won't align. But to mix metaphors, it is good to get as many ducks in a row as you can. If you want to start, why not give it a go? Your toddler may surprise you by how ready he is.

You still have some decisions to make and preparation to do, so check out the next couple of chapters before you launch in.

ACTION ITEM – Decide When to Start

Start observing signs of readiness in your toddler, and then decide on a good time to start.

CHAPTER EIGHT

Decisions

Decisions to Make

You have settled on some basic goals, determined your child is ready to be toilet trained, and are in the process of psyching yourself up to be supercalifragilistically positive, patient and chillaxed.

But you still have a number of decisions to make. It is good to decide these things in advance so you have a better idea of how you want to proceed. You can change your mind, but getting clarity about some key aspects of toilet training up front will set you on the path to success.

Names

You have probably decided on acceptable toilet talk language well before this time, but if you haven't, do so now.

Determine the Date to Start

The toilet training process in this book starts off with a few days of intense focus for which you need to be at home with your toddler and have very few distractions. Usually the start of an upcoming quiet weekend is a good time. Lock that into your diary.

Daytime versus Nighttime

It needs to be decided whether you are going to focus on just daytime toilet training or try to take your child out of diapers at night as well. Nighttime training has its own set of considerations. For the purposes of this book, it is assumed you will split up the toilet training and only focus on daytime training first. If you want to try nighttime training at the same time, read that chapter, too.

Potty or Toilet?

I bet your dazzling younger self never thought that one day you would be reading a book to help you to decide between a potty and a toilet. Yes, this is what your life has become, and you wouldn't have it any other way.

An entire book could be written on the merits of using a potty versus using a toilet. Some people are entirely in one camp and others ferociously defend the other. With potties you can decide to have only one that is placed in the toilet or bathroom area, or perhaps start off with a few scattered around the house for easy access. With toilets you need to decide whether you buy an insert that you can take in and out or a whole new toilet seat that incorporates a permanent smaller seat inside the lid.

You can change your mind or adapt to suit your child and your circumstances. Also you can use a combination of the two. This has the potential to be the best of both worlds or create more confusion. Actually, please do not spend too long on this, as whatever you have settled on, your child will decide that she likes the other.

Eventually, of course, your child needs to know how to use a big person toilet so this decision is just for this transitional phase, which can be weeks or months long. Remember your goals; you don't want to send him off to high school with his own potty.

In the interest of trying to keep this brief, I have created a table.

Type	Pros	Cons
Potty	Inexpensive – basic ones only cost a few dollars Comfortable - the right size and easy to use for little bottoms Separate - only for the child Convenient – doesn't have to be in the bathroom Accessible - can have a few placed around the house Reachable - may be easier to get to (especially if you only have one toilet in the house) Portable - can take potty out of the house (familiar and convenient) Relatively easy to clean Possibly safer	More work - you have to tip the contents into toilet and clean the potty afterwards. Your child may only want to do business in the potty and not transition to the toilet well (in and out of the house). If you start with potties in places other than the bathroom, she may not learn to go in the correct place.
Toilet with	Avoids any possible	Using a toilet needs more

a separate insert or a hinged seat	problems of transitioning from a potty to a toilet and not being able to use a toilet while out of the home	adult supervision than a potty as it is higher
		No splashguards on some models mean boys while seated have to be extra vigilant to pee downwards
	Less cleaning required as you just need to flush	Guests may be confused with the new toilet set up
	More discreet and neater than a potty	Insert only – may be inconvenient and cause a time delay to take insert in and out of toilet seat each time
	Insert only – can take out of the house to use	Hinged seat only – more expensive
	Hinged seat only - Less stuff in bathroom and feels more grown up	Hinged seat only – permanent so if renting or going to move house then perhaps not an option

Underpants, Training Pants or Pull-Ups

In the olden days you went from diapers to underwear. Nowadays things have gotten more complicated. You can now buy 'training pants' that are washable, like underpants, but more absorbent – they look bigger on. You can also buy 'pull-ups,' which are like disposable diapers but easier to get on and off. Very cleverly, both these types of pants are able to absorb some pee but also let a child feel some dampness. They also contain number twos much better than underpants.

I bet your dazzling younger self never thought.... yes, yes, same as above. And I repeat what I said above – this might only be important in the initial stages of toilet training. Eventually the tiny human needs to get used to wearing real underpants.

What should you choose? Most parents I talked to started with underpants at home but kept some pull-ups or diapers on hand for naptime and trips out and about, at least at first. Here is another table.

Type	Pros	Cons
Underpants	Your child feels like there is a real change happening as they feel quite different from diapers Underpants reinforce your toddler being a 'big kid now' - more grown up If there is an accident, your child feels uncomfortable faster and so makes connections more quickly	Accidents that occur in their underpants are not well contained
Training Pants (absorbable, washable	Easy and less stress Less cleaning required as accidents are captured	Both types are more expensive than underpants

underpants) or Pull-Ups (disposable, easy to get up and down diapers)	Still feel a bit wet, so getting the connections A step away from diapers Training pants only - more environmentally friendly than diapers and pull-ups Training pants only - hard-wearing and washable Pull-ups only - can just throw away	Your child may not make connections as fast as they are not that different from wearing a diaper Your child may not gain the motivation to go to the potty as she knows deposits will be contained and you will just change them Training pants only – still have to wash them Pull-ups only – can only use once

With regard to underpants, there are a couple of things to note:

- Buy 20 or 30 cheap pairs knowing that some underpants will be thrown away if there are particularly nasty accidents.
- Make sure some of the pairs are in the next size up in case your toddler grows fast.
- Try to get some with a picture on the front so that it is easy to see which way round they go.
- An optional extra is to buy a few pairs of branded underpants as a bit of a reward and possibly to encourage fewer accidents.

Mama Tip - My daughter chose Disney Princess knickers and we talked about not peeing on the princesses! - Collette

Decision Muscles

This chapter has started to develop your decision-making muscles, and by the end of the book you will be a professional weight lifter in the decision-making category.

ACTION ITEM – Make Some Decisions
Decide on:

- Names for all the 'toilet talk' (if you haven't already)
- A good date to start
- Whether you will focus only on daytime training at first or incorporate night training at the same time
- Whether you are going to use a potty, the toilet or both
- Whether you will use underpants, training pants, pull-ups or a combination

CHAPTER NINE
Be Prepared

Toilet Training Preparation

You have set some goals, made some decisions, decided the stars have aligned as much as they can and you are chomping at the bit, rearing to go. But hold on there, partner, you have to follow the Scouts motto here and 'Be Prepared'.

The Toileting Process

If you step back and think about it, going to the toilet is actually quite a complex and lengthy process. Somehow, we expect our two-year-olds to become experts at it in a short period of time. Could you drive a car perfectly after only a couple of lessons?

Going to the Toilet – The Process:

- Recognize the body signal that indicates you want to go.
- Get to the toilet or bathroom or where the potty is.
- Get clothes and underpants down or off.
- Do your business and make sure you're completely finished.
- Wipe your bottom with toilet paper.
- Dispose of toilet paper appropriately.
- Pull underpants back up and clothes on.
- Put the lid down and flush the toilet.

- Wash hands with soap and water and dry them thoroughly.

This pre-work helps your toddler to get familiar with all of these steps and start to understand the order around going to the toilet.

Tasks Before You Actually Start

There are a few tasks you can do before the real potty training begins that help your child get used to the whole 'going to the toilet' idea. A lot of these may just develop naturally anyway. This lays the groundwork for making going to the toilet a normal part of the day.

1. Let him see you going to the toilet (as if you could keep him out of there before). This helps him see the whole complex process in all its glory.
2. As she is watching you going to the toilet anyway, talk to her about what you are doing. Not actually what you are *doing*, but statements like, "Mommy is flushing the toilet now and then Mommy is going to wash her hands," help your tot see the order of things.
3. Talk to your child. Yes, this simple step is often missed. Tell him he is not a baby any more and he is getting to be a big boy. Part of that is using the toilet. Clearly state your intention to start toilet training. Give him some warning that change is going to happen.
4. Talk to significant others in your life and tell them you will be potty training your child soon. This includes your partner, other children in the family, grandparents and teachers at the childcare center or kindergarten. Enlist their help if appropriate (see more on this later).

Optional Extras

Your main goal is to make going to the toilet normal. However, to get your little one happy with the change, sometimes it is a good idea to make it not only normal but fun and enjoyable. Up the excitement factor, especially if you expect a higher level of resistance with your child. Choose to do some or all of these if you think it will help:

1. Get your child to practice sitting on the potty or the toilet with her diapers still on.

2. Show her what sitting on the potty or toilet looks like with dolls or soft toys, and get her to role-play. There are even 'proper' dolls that you can buy that squirt out 'pee' and even number twos (yes, really). Or some parents make their own deposits with lemon water and strained prunes. I am not kidding you. Now, trust your gut on this one, if you think 'yuck', then don't do it, but if you feel like this will help your child's understanding, then role-play away.

3. Start with one habitual potty sitting time for a few weeks before the real potty training begins. A good time is just before he gets in the bath. Encourage your toddler to sit on the potty and see if any pee comes. At the very least this may keep the bath cleaner for longer.

4. Read children's picture books about going on the potty. There are a surprising abundance of these. Search your library.

5. Make the business area inviting. Having a warm and comfortable spot is a good start. Some families encourage the child to decorate the potty with a few stickers (it is now a princess throne or a racing car!) You can add pictures on the walls or place a mirror in front of him

(toddlers love looking at themselves) to encourage him to sit there. Perhaps add books to read or toys play with or as an 'audience' for your child. Add what you think is appropriate but do not go overboard. You want him to stay there long enough to do his business but not spend all day in there.

Shopping

Go shopping! Yes it is for a few dull items such as potties, cleaning equipment and underpants, but it is an essential part of the preparation.

Take your child with you and make a big deal out of it. This is another way to get her understanding and even excited about the upcoming changes.

If the budget allows, you can even get her to help choose some of the items. She might like a particular color of potty or a special design on underpants. If the thought of bringing your child along stresses you out, then don't do it, it is up to you.

Shopping List - Recommended

- about 20 or 30 pairs of kids underpants (with a picture on the front)
- potty or potties
- a new toilet seat or toilet seat insert
- a small footstool or step (used to get up to the toilet, rest little feet on while on the toilet or to stand by the wash basin)
- anti-bacterial hand soap

- toilet paper and perhaps flushable bottom wipes
- cleaning supplies for accidents such as rubber gloves, paper towels, cleaning wipes, cloths or sponges, a mop, a bucket, disinfectant, carpet cleaner, detergent and stain remover (see the "Accidents Happen" chapter later)

Shopping List - Optional

- training pants (washable)
- pull-ups (disposable)
- 'branded' underpants (for example with a favorite Disney character on the front)
- stickers or small low-value toys for rewards (see the "Incentives and Rewards" chapter later)
- a little notebook to record those gems (if you haven't already)

Congratulations ... on Not Starting Yet

You have set some goals, decided a time to start, decided on the ins and outs of how you want to proceed and gone shopping. Phew, how exhausting, and you haven't even started yet. Yes you could just jump in the deep end and not go through all these steps. But you are here and now you are much more prepared for what is coming next.

ACTION ITEM – Go Shopping

CHAPTER TEN

Stage One - The Short Intense Period

The Vital Step

The consensus from modern parents and the approach in this book is to have a few days of dedicated focus on potty training. Follow this with an active maintenance period of a couple of weeks to a couple of months in which toilet training is at the forefront. In the third stage it becomes just another part of daily life.

This strategy is to get your child fully toilet trained at daytime only. See the "Nighttime" chapter to incorporate that part during one of the three stages, or afterwards.

Please do NOT skip this first 'short intense period' stage. It is of immense value to help cement the brain connections around going to the toilet. You have made many decisions so far, so just surrender to the wisdom of the majority here.

However, by the end of the short period it is <u>extremely</u> unlikely that your child will be 100% toilet trained. The truth is, most children take months to be fully daytime toilet trained, but "Potty Train in Three Months" is not going to be a best seller.

The Short Intense Period

You have been chomping at the bit for a while now. Time to let you off the leash. Run free. Go!

Mark off a few days in your calendar when you and your child are going to stay at home all day. Do not leave your property, don't plan to have visitors over, and no short visits to the store. No work, no daycare. If it helps, pretend there is a zombie apocalypse outside your house.

This apocalyptic situation also extends to how you conduct yourself inside the house. You want to be almost attached by the hip to your toddler. Hovering has bad connotations these days, but just try to be near him at all times. You are not a drill sergeant, but you don't want to disappear either. You are there to observe, give a helping hand and aid the transition.

You also need to prearrange a lot of activities that you can do together. You don't want anything too stimulating, as she may get too involved in what she is doing and forget about going toilet. This also helps keep your attention on your child.

Imagine, just you and your toddler reading books, doing puzzles, drawing pictures, sculpting play-dough, building block towers, gardening or baking. You could spend some time outside with water play, blowing bubbles or playing with a ball. You may actually enjoy yourself and feel even closer to your wonderful child. There is something so whimsical about giving your toddler your sole attention and interacting with old-fashioned activities. Cherish this precious time together.

This means that beforehand your laundry is as up-to-date as it ever will be, dinners are pre-cooked (or someone else is bringing home takeaways), and the vacuum cleaner remains in the cupboard. If you really cannot imagine not doing any chores, then enlist your sidekick as a little helper. He can help you cook dinner, hang out the washing or do some jobs that have been sitting on the list for a while, like cleaning out the pantry (he will LOVE that one).

Therefore, you should have (shock, horror) NO screen time. No phones, no computers, no TV for either of you. That way you both will not get too engrossed in the screen and forget about toilet training. I don't want to lose you on this, so if that is too hard, wait until after the tiny human has gone to bed to check emails, binge watch your favorite program or get your fix of cat videos.

How Many Days?

So to the great question - how many days does this take? Use some common sense around your decision here. More than one day helps to cement learning. If you really cannot take time off work, at the minimum the two full days over a weekend could suffice. At the other end, a maximum of a week at home is recommended. Any more than that and you could go a bit batty being stuck at home having to do a happy dance every time your toddler pees in the potty.

Hence three or four days are ideal. Many parents choose a weekend when a statutory holiday is tacked on or they are able to get some leave. It won't be the most exciting long weekend you have ever had, but you are a parent now, so suck it up.

Mama Tip – Stay home while training! We took my poor son to the zoo while he was potty training (the first round) and that was a disaster for all of us. We did a few more day activities too. Dumb! Don't! - Annabelle

Do I Get Others Involved?

The ideal rule here is that if you can get other significant people 100% on board with the toilet training plan, then keep them around. If they are going to be more of a hindrance, then send them away.

Now practicalities play a part of course. If there are older siblings to take care of, can your partner take the main responsibility for them while you focus on toilet training? Maybe Grandma can take them for the weekend or your partner can take them away for a break. Or if that is not possible, then maybe Grandma can come and stay and keep an eye on the older kids while you and your partner take turns with potty training duty.

The most important thing is to minimize distractions for the one in the middle of toilet training, so work out the most realistic way you can do that.

Day One

On the first day of the short intense period, go through your morning routine as usual. With the first diaper change, put on proper underwear instead of the diaper. Explain to your child that he is now wearing big boy undies. If he feels like he needs to go to the toilet, he needs to tell you. He will most likely look like he hasn't understood a word of what you just said, but the explanation is important. A lot more goes in than you realize.

It is probably easiest for her and you if she only wears underpants and no other trousers, skirts or shorts. Of course when you get back to normal daily life and the real world, this will change, but for the sake of your blood pressure, and washing powder, just let her run around in undies for a few days. More often than not, she will love it.

She can even have no underpants. A lot of parents notice that having no underwear helps their children pick up the fact that they are wetting themselves much quicker and therefore helps the toilet training move along faster.

During the day, offer him water as you normally would. He does not need to drink additional amounts just because he is being potty trained. Offer him a cup here and there and around meal times so that he averages about two pints or one liter per day. If you want to give a bit of variety to the liquid intake, then offer ice blocks, watermelon, sparkling water, water with lemon juice, coconut water or milk as alternatives.

Tell and Bring

About half an hour after breakfast, say to your toddler that she is to go on the potty or to the toilet. She is likely to say 'No', ignore you or have no idea what you are talking about.

At this point, take her by the hand to the bathroom and invite her to sit on the potty or toilet. Doing this is a gentle reminder that the potty or toilet is there for her to use and that sometimes activities need to be interrupted for short periods to do her business. If she doesn't want to sit, a good way to encourage her is to say "Maybe the pee is hiding."

For this short intense period, you are not asking him whether he needs to go. You are not even leaving it up to him to take himself. You are telling him, "Its time for a pee," and escorting. Firmly and gently. You won't be doing this for a long time. In the active maintenance period, you can ask or remind, but this stage is all about getting connections, normalizing the process and making it part of the routine of the day. So usher him into the bathroom and sit him on the potty.

Every hour or two tell him he probably needs to go to the toilet or potty and escort him there. At natural breaks in the day – before meals, naptime and bath time - also tell him it's time to go and sit on the potty. This makes it a routine part of the day. You can get really involved in how often and when you should take your little one. Some books talk about using a timer to buzz a reminder and perhaps recording visits in a notebook or a chart, but you probably do not need to go that far.

For extra bonus points, this is where you can start to check for signals that they are needing to go you learned previously – wriggling, dancing, silence, escaping to behind the couch. If you manage to notice anything of the sort, say, "Potty now" and take her to it. You will not have a lot of time. A combination of toilet breaks in the daily routine and watching for signals is the ideal approach.

Rinse and repeat. You will feel like you are talking to him 100 times a day about going toilet. You will get sick of repeating yourself. He will probably get sick of you talking about it. But this is all part of the learning and a necessary part of this time. You may even see some pattern developing so you can predict best times to suggest a pee stop. This would be an amazing outcome.

Praise and Patience

Be very generous with praise in the first few days, even if he sits on the toilet and nothing happens. What does praise and encouragement look like? It can be whatever you want it to be. Here are a few suggestions:

- Give her a smile, cuddles, hugs, kisses, a high-five or a pat on the back.
- Say things like "Well done," "You're being a big boy," or "Great try."
- Clap your hands (you may feel ridiculous).
- Do a happy dance (it goes without saying you will feel ridiculous).
- Sing a special song (made up songs about poo, pee and bottoms are especially rewarding for a two-year-old).

Mama Story - We made up a song, kind of like the conga, for a successful toilet trip. "Daisy peed on the po-TTY, Daisy peed on the po-TTY. We would sing it coming out of the bathroom so that anyone around would know and as a bit of a celebration! - Marianne

Get ready to be patient. It may feel like eternity waiting for him on the toilet. A good trick is to count to 20 slowly or sing a nursery rhyme song to yourself. If nothing has happened after that, then encourage him to get off the potty and move on to something else.

Some children want to do their business quickly and get out, and others happily sit there for hours on end, especially if there is a book to read or toys to play with. Work out a happy medium with which you are all comfortable. Do not force her to stay on longer than two to five minutes. If nothing has happened by then, it is not likely to.

Accident Scenarios

Sooner or later, despite all the reminders and bathroom breaks, your toddler will have a pee accident. How this plays out will determine your response.

Scenario 1)

She gets a feeling that she wants to go and either tells you and you both try to get to the toilet, or she moves towards the toilet by herself. You may or may not make it in time. This would be a premium gold-star outcome. Praise your child extensively.

A note on the 'scoop and run'. If your toddler tells you he needs to go, or your super-sleuth powers notice severe jiggling, then you may have, at the most, five seconds before his bladder starts to empty. (This message will self-destruct in 5, 4…). If you are close to the bathroom and not faint of heart, then scooping up your toddler and running to the nearest commode may be a good strategy. However, if you are far away from the toilet or potty you may just have to let the accident happen and deal with cleaning up after. It's probably better to wait until she is finished for number twos.

Afterwards, always take her over to the potty. Say something neutral like, "Pee goes in the potty." Get her to sit on the potty. Oftentimes there may be a little bit more pee that then goes in the potty. This is a little win in an otherwise not fun situation.

Scenario 2)

He has an accident and notices it. At some point, liquid appears down his leg or on the floor. He may be distressed or curious. Give him some empathy and explain what happened. Something short along the lines of, "Oh look, you had an accident. It's okay, Mommy will clean it. Next time we will go to the toilet." Sit him on the potty like before and see if there is any more pee. Then calmly clean him up, sort out new clothes and clean the floor. (See the "Accidents Happen" chapter for more here). Remind him to tell you if he wants to go to the toilet in future. Carry on with your puzzle/blocks/cleaning the pantry out.

Scenario 3)

She has her first accident and doesn't notice it. This is the less than optimum scenario and could mean that she is not ready for potty training. But don't throw in the towel just yet. This is why you have given yourself three days. She needs to start to make linkages in her brain, and the only way she is going to do that is by learning on the job. Repeat your response per the above scenarios and hopefully sooner or later she at least notices an accident happening.

Mama Story - My friend Shelley wanted to give up, but sat down after the third night and had a very large gin and resolved to give it another go. The next day her son didn't have a single accident. So... if in doubt or desperation, try gin. - Louise

Daytime Naps

For naps, encourage her to sit on the toilet or potty first, then put on a diaper or pull-up. To avoid confusion say something like, "You might not realize you are peeing when you are sleeping, so you can have diapers on for your nap." If you are at all worried about her being confused, change to a pull-up or a different diaper brand, but really, children know when there are different scenarios in play. It does not matter if she wakes up with a wet diaper, just change her out of it when she gets up and carry on as before.

"Wipe My Bottom!"

Does she wipe her own bottom or do you do it? Most parents weigh up the choice between the inconvenience and general drudgery of wiping their child's bottom versus allowing the child to wipe her own and finding (later) that she has not done a good enough job. Most choose the first option, at least at the beginning.

What If There is No Poop?

By the end of the first few days, you could be faced with a situation in which you haven't seen a bowel movement. This is more common than you may think. It will come eventually, so the main thing is don't worry about it. Keep up the fluids and high-fiber nutritious food. Create a relaxed environment and say things like the 'poop will slide out' to emphasize how easy it will be to do number twos. Praise any attempts even if nothing eventuates at the time. You will see a bowel movement again even if you move on to Stage Two without one.

Mama Tip – A sugary snack (sweets or dried fruit) and quiet play with an interesting toy – guarantees a poo every time. - Raewyn

Cleaning the Potty

If he is going in the potty, you need to empty it into the toilet. After tipping out the contents, wash the potty with cold water. With number twos, in particular, spray some disinfectant around it as well. (It goes without saying that you need to keep the disinfectant on hand but out of reach of the little one). Dry the potty with an old towel that you only use for these kinds of tasks.

Daddy Tip – This is not the time to play tickle games or jump out from behind a curtain games – unless you want to clean up accidents! - Rob

The End of Stage One

By the end of day three (or however many days your have assigned to the intense period), your toddler should be somewhere on the toilet training continuum between not understanding at all what is going on and being able to detect a need to go signal and getting to a potty or toilet to do his business in time.

If there are issues, delve into the problems and solutions section to get them resolved and then decide your next plan of action. If there are still a few accidents but your little one seems to be catching on to the whole idea, then carry on with toilet training – go to Stage Two.

ACTION ITEM – Do the short intense period of toilet training for a few days. DO NOT SKIP THIS STEP!! See you on the other side.

CHAPTER ELEVEN
Stage Two - The Active Maintenance Period

After the First Few Days

Congratulations, you have made it through the first stage. Now you and your child have to rejoin the real world. No more zombie apocalypse. No more just wearing underpants (or going commando). No more exclusive focus just on toilet training.

In this period, your child may be resuming childcare arrangements outside the home (see the "Childcare" chapter) and going out with you to run errands, for fun or to visit people (see the "Out and About" chapter). Around the home, toilet training is still a major part of day-to-day life but is woven into daily routines.

The big question is how long do you have to keep this relaxed vigilance up? It is hard work! The length of the active maintenance period is different for everyone, but on average put it at couple of weeks to a couple of months. Don't let this get you down, some days may feel like they drag on but the time will pass quickly. This stage comes with its own set of challenges, and you may feel like things slide back a little. If this happens, remind yourself of your goals and how great it will be when your little one is fully toilet trained.

Keys to Successful Potty Training

It's good to keep in mind the keys to successful potty training – repetition, consistency, positivity, and patience as well as the ability to quickly assess your toddler's needs.

Repetition:
Saying things like "Tell Daddy if you need to go," "Remember your potty is there if you need to go," and "You are a big girl so you wear underpants now" are second nature to you now.

Consistency:
Get into some good patterns in your day-to-day life. At minimum, remind him about going to the toilet before meal breaks, at bedtime and before leaving the house.

Positivity:
This involves anything from a simple "Well done" to a happy dance. If things don't go to plan, then positivity is even more important: "Don't worry about the accident, you will do better next time."

Mama Story - Leigh made her grandparents and aunties watch her pee on the potty and then she made them all clap for her - Collette

Patience:
From waiting for her to do anything on the potty to keeping it together when she throws toilet paper all over the house, this is a learning period and patience is essential.

Mama or Daddy Detective
You are honing your super-sleuth skills and noticing that that small

hip movement is actually a sign that he needs to go. You still need to be quick here and say "Toilet now" or do the 'scoop and run'.

Tell or Ask?

In the active maintenance period there is less requirement to escort her to the toilet. If you notice any 'pee dance' signs, then tell her to go to the toilet. The rest of the time say, "Remember to tell Mommy if you want to go pee," or "Why don't you see if the pee is hiding?" You may have picked up on some patterns when your child is likely to go, so marry those up to your reminders.

If he says 'No' or ignores you, prompt him about the potty and then leave it. Say, "I can see you need to go for a pee - the potty is there." Then move away.

It is a bit of a tightrope act to balance watchfulness with supposed nonchalance, but it's a necessary step in the right direction. Don't rush the self-initiation part; it comes in its own time. You can count on prompting for a good three weeks.

Here is a sample of things you can say to your tot to encourage her to go.

- You can do it, you just need to try.
- Have you got any pee waiting or hiding?
- I need to hear more pee.
- Let's see if we can catch a pee or poo in the toilet.
- Your tummy might be feeling full or a little bit sore.
- Let the poo slide out.
- Open up your poop gate.

Daytime Naps

You may want to switch to underpants at naptimes. If she is waking up dry after her nap, then give this a try. Alternatively, give it say two weeks and make a change. Regardless of whether she is in a crib or a bed, put a waterproof covering on the mattress. Explain to her the change and see what happens.

"Wipe My Bottom!"

At this stage, you may be wiping her bottom all the time. Alternatively, your child may start it and you could do a final follow through. Sooner or later she needs to be able to wipe her own bottom properly. See above regarding going off to high school.

I am well aware I promised at the beginning that I would treat you as an adult and not, for instance, tell you how to wash your hands. This does extend also to bottom wiping, with which I am sure you have much experience. However, there are three things about wiping that need to be taught to your little one:

- How much toilet paper he should pull off to wipe (not the whole roll!)
- For number twos he should wipe until he can see no more marks on the toilet paper.
- Girls must wipe front to back to form healthy habits.

Mama Story - After going poo on the toilet, Alicia calls out that she is finished. If we are delayed, she hits the wall and counts until we get there. She counts in a funny way. While hitting the wall, "one, two, three, four, twelve, sixteen, eleventen". I think we still need to work on our numbers. She asks me every time if I heard her count! Bizarre. - Zoe

Where Should He Be At the End of Stage Two?

If you have scattered potties all over the house, you may want to start moving them to the bathroom and getting down to one potty. After a while you can tell if your child can make it to the bathroom or toilet. This is discussed more in Stage Three (along with transitioning to the toilet), but know that it is an option during this time, too.

You know you are at the end of Stage Two when:

- Your child recognizes signals that he needs to go pee and poo.
- She can tell you she needs to go and enlists your help, or gets to the potty or toilet by herself.
- You still remind him about going but this becomes less of a chore.
- She is getting better at the other parts of toileting – wiping her own bottom, pulling up her pants and washing her hands
- He is fairly consistently dry during daytime naps and short outings.
- There are a few accidents but they are not an everyday occurrence.

If you are having some difficulties in various areas (for example, you may notice that your child pees in the potty or toilet just fine but you cannot for all the gold in the world get a bowel movement in the correct place), then check out the problems and solutions section.

However, if your child displays most of the things on the above list, then you have pretty much made it. Toilet training has worked. Move onto Stage Three, the longest but easiest stage.

ACTION ITEM –

- Hone your super-sleuth skills and relaxed vigilance skills by only reminding your toddler when you notice signals he needs to go.
- Attempt daytime naps without a diaper or pull-up.
- Encourage more independence by, for example, letting her start the bottom wiping process and washing her own hands.

CHAPTER TWELVE

Stage Three - Toilet Training Over The Long Term

After a While

After a month or two, all going well, there are fewer accidents, less need to repeatedly remind your tot to go and some progress on toileting in the right order. Stage Three can last until high school, but after a few months it mostly fades into the background of your daily life.

During this stage, your main task is to keep up the super-duper parenting aspects that you invoked in Stages One and Two. Keep up the consistency, positivity and patience but tone down the repetition. Allow your child to cement learning her own body signals and self-initiate going to the toilet. Use your detective abilities. When you notice the tell-tale 'pee-pee dance' tell her that she may want to go and sit on the toilet as the pee is coming or just say "Potty. Now."

Toilet Skills Mastery

Here is a list of toilet training skills that your little one should master over this longer period:

- Wants to wear underpants (not diapers)
- Aware that he is wet or dirty or had an accident (past)

- Can say when going pee or poo (present)
- Knows what the 'need to go' feels like (future)
- Remembers to go and sit on potty or toilet
- Able take pants off and on by himself
- Can go pee/poo (including wiping her bottom) with little or no help
- Will flush the toilet
- Will wash and dry his hands

Daytime Naps

By now, your child should not have diapers on for his nap. Make sure it is a normal part of the daily routine to sit on the potty just before naptime. More often than not he should wake up dry, but have a waterproof mattress protector on the crib or bed just in case. See more about mattress protectors in the "Nighttime" chapter.

"Wipe My Bottom!"

You may have to wipe his bottom for quite some time, especially for number twos, but the day that he has gone without you even realizing is a happy day indeed. You may wonder whether he wiped himself properly (or washed his hands at all), but do a little happy dance on your way to asking him.

Privacy

By this stage, some children still might want you to stay by them (on the potty or the toilet) while they do their business and others may tell you to go. This is one of the smaller details that works out over time. Do you trust her not to put the entire toilet roll down the toilet/ repeatedly flush/ not flush at all in your absence? Or is it okay if she does not get these details right every time? If she wants privacy, then leave her to it. After all, do you like anyone staring at you while you do your business? Note that this applies at home only – using public toilets involves more considerations. See the "Out and About" chapter for more.

Moving to The Toilet

The main question in Stage Three is when and how to start using the toilet. There are a few steps to this.

If your child is using a number of potties scattered around the house, the first thing to do is direct him to use one potty situated in the bathroom or toilet room (if it is separate from the bathroom). It really doesn't matter which room you choose, just get down to one potty in the general vicinity of the actual toilet.

This may happen after a few days or may take months. Most of the time you can tell when it is a good time to get down to one potty. The first indicator is that there are more than one or two seconds between the realization of pee coming and when it actually comes. Another clue is that while there are two or three potties around the house, only one is being used regularly.

Alternatively, just set yourself a date and hide the rest of the potties, leaving just one in the bathroom. There may be a bit of resistance at first, but you probably won't have much of an issue.

Next, start encouraging your child to use the toilet. You will have more success at this if you make it easy to access, comfortable to use and reduce any fears around it. Make sure it is easy to access by offering a footstool to step up to the toilet. This is also good for resting his feet on so he is more relaxed on the toilet. Then ensure the toilet is comfortable to sit on by using a toilet insert or smaller hinged permanent seat.

Daddy Tip - If your child can't reach the toilet roll, buy a cheap second one that suctions onto the wall to use until their arms get longer. - James

If there is still some opposition to using the toilet, try any of the following ideas:

- Introduce using the toilet as part of the daily routine, for example just before bathtime.
- Allow a two-stage process in which poo still happens on the potty but pee goes into the toilet (or even vice versa).
- Tell her she is a big kid so she gets to use the toilet now.
- For boys, tell him he can stand up to pee in the toilet, just like Daddy.
- Remind her that she uses the toilet when at daycare or out of the house (if that is the case).
- Encourage him to access the toilet in his own way, at least at first – for instance, some children love sitting on the toilet backward (koala style), as hugging the toilet makes them feel safer (yes, really).
- Or simply go cold turkey, remove the potty and tell your child the toilet is the place to be. Sometimes this causes more problems, but if everything else you have tried is not working then why not try it?

If your child appears panicked or distraught, then he may have some real fears or worries about using the toilet. These may seem ridiculous to you, but they are obviously preventing your child from progressing up to using the toilet, so they need to be taken seriously. If you suspect that this is the case, check out the problems and solutions section for help.

Congratulations – You Have Made It

Your toddler is now fully toilet trained at daytime. What a fantastic achievement! With a little bit of planning and preparation outlined in this book, the transition was smooth and much less stressful than you thought it would be. Read on for information about cleaning up accidents, what to do with childcare or when you are out and about.

ACTION ITEM – Encourage using the toilet and store the potty away.

CHAPTER THIRTEEN
Accidents Happen

Cleaning Up Accidents

Like death and taxes, accidents during toilet training are guaranteed. You will not get through potty training without at least one accident. Therefore, an extremely low expectation of your success at first, and a high expectation of cleaning up accidents will put you in the right mindset.

Put away any expensive rugs or floor mats that you would like to keep pristine. (I am not sure why anyone would have these with very young children, but it is worth mentioning just in case). And if you are thinking of replacing the carpet, do so after this developmental stage. Keep your stress levels low from the outset.

Your Approach

Your child's reaction to an accident can vary from not being aware, to being curious or distressed, or anything in between. Regardless of her response, it is <u>your</u> approach that matters.

It is very important to remind yourself that your child is almost never having an accident on purpose to annoy you. If you really believe that he is going pee or poop away from the potty on purpose, check out the problems section for solutions.

Here are your 'DOs' and the one big 'DON'T' for all accidents:

- DO be calm, quiet, resolute, matter of fact, neutral – you *are* Switzerland.
- DO act slightly positive, even jovial or light-hearted.
- DO show love, kindness and reassurance.
- DO tidy up the mess quickly and without fuss.
- DO tell her to tell you when she needs to use the potty or take her there and explain to her again that we pee/poop in potty/toilet and we have to keep our knickers dry.

- DON'T reprimand, shame, get angry at him, show frustration or punish him in any way.

Suggested Things to Say

Here are some things you can say when an accident happens. Feel free to use any of these sound bites:

- 'Don't worry darling, these things happen when you first start to use the toilet, it's not a big deal.'
- 'It's okay, you will get there next time.'
- 'Nevermind, woopsee, come on let's get you changed.'
- 'No worries love, you just need to remember to take a break from playing and go sooner next time.'
- 'It's okay, no worries, I'll clean it up.'
- 'Uh oh! Remember, pee-pee goes in the potty.'

Tools and Strategy

It helps to have the right tools on hand and a strategy to deal with accidents. The tools that you need are:

- cleaning products including disinfectant
- a bucket or two or an old container
- paper towels, wipes, sponges, old towels
- (optional) – rubber gloves, a mop

Your strategy differs between a pee or poop accident but basically:

- If possible take your child and sit her on the potty/toilet to remind her of what she should do.
- Remove soiled clothes from your child.
- Clean up your child.
- Clean up yourself, if necessary.
- Clean up the floor and any other area involved.

Cleaning Up – Them, You and Clothes

You will be a pro in no time at cleaning up pee only accidents. They really are not a big deal. Urine is actually very sterile. Poo is a bit more 'icky'. If you are particularly lucky, the stools will be well formed and captured in your toddler's underpants. In this case try to get the underpants off and tip the contents into the toilet. Tell your little one, "Poo goes in here."

After his underpants are off, put him on the potty or toilet to see if there is any more pee or poo. Go through the 'normal' toilet process – wipe bottom, flush, wash hands.

Then sponge him down with a cloth or a wet wipe, dry him with a towel and find him some new underpants to put on. Tidy yourself up if required (if, for instance, the 'scoop and run' didn't work very well).

Put his wet underpants straight into the washing machine ready for the next wash, or in a bucket to soak. If it is a bad poop accident, instead of trying to soak out the stains in underpants, consider just throwing them away. It is not the best for the landfill, but it is quite good for your blood pressure. This is why you bought so many pairs of underpants in the first place. If you really want to save the underpants, then tip out what you can in the toilet, wash out the extra bad bits and leave the underwear to soak for a few hours in a bucket with some washing powder before putting in the washing machine.

Cleaning Up – The Floor or Other Areas

Then clean the floor. Remove any excess poop and put it in the toilet. If the accident is on wooden floor or linoleum, use paper towels, a sponge or a mop to clean it and dry with an old towel. On carpet, soak up excess moisture (from pee) with paper towels or a sponge. Then put some cold or lukewarm (not hot) water on the area and soak up the water with a towel. Press down firmly or stand on the towel. If you are annoyed at all, this is a good time to let it out by stomping on the towel on the wet floor. If you are worried about stains or smells, then some natural cleaners such as baking soda or a little bit of white vinegar mixed with water can work. You could use some disinfectant mixed with water (such as one used for pet accidents), but check cleaning instructions first.

If the accident is not on the floor, say it is on the sofa or a kitchen chair, then use water and a natural or chemical disinfectant. Afterwards upholstery cleaner may be needed. Check all instructions or spot test first. With a highchair or a car seat, usually parts are removable and can be cleaned separately.

Last But Not Least

The main thing to remember with accidents is although they seem like a big deal at the time, you tend to forget about them after a while. You can always splurge out on a professional carpet clean after the main potty training period is over, or even consider replacing the carpets if they were old in the first place.

Remind yourself that it is just stuff. So please try not to show your tiny human a negative reaction to an accident. Being toilet trained is much less important than a solid, trusting and happy relationship.

ACTION ITEM – Stock up on cleaning supplies and a positive mindset.

CHAPTER FOURTEEN

Childcare Outside The Home

Childcare Considerations

During Stage Two you may need to integrate outside childcare with potty training. However, you need to make some decisions and plan a few things in advance.

Childcare outside the home is called many things and comes in many forms. From utilizing the grandparents, to daycare, kindergarten, crèche, nursery or preschool, childcare outside the home can be your best friend or worst enemy during toilet training.

Some childcare centers have professional staff who are qualified and experienced in how to toilet train children. Other places either want a child still in diapers or one who is fully toilet trained and do not want the responsibility of potty training. Figure out which type your provider falls under and make some decisions from there.

If They Are Helpful

Hopefully your child is at a daycare whose staff are pros at how to toilet train. Even if they are not as experienced, for instance, if the grandparents are minding your child, they can still be on board with the whole thing with some notice.

The best way to work together is to tell them of your plans to toilet train your child. Tell them the start date and ask them if they have a policy or particular approach on toilet training. Tell them what you want from them and what they should expect. For instance you may not want them to put diapers on unless absolutely necessary.

Questions to ask them include:

- What is their policy? Have they got a written copy for you?
- What should you pack in the daycare bag for accidents?
- Should you bring some diapers, training pants or pull-ups in as well?
- Do they ask children if they need to go and encourage at certain times of the day (eg: before meals)?
- What do they do if there is an accident?
- Do they let parents know if there have been accidents during the day or do they record them?
- Do they have their own potties, allow potties to be brought from home, or do children only go on the toilet?

Mama Story - Our son Dylan moved daycare providers during the first few weeks of toilet training. His first daycare center allowed us to bring in his own potty. The second daycare had a 'no potties' rule. At both places the toilets were the appropriate level for little bodies and he got used to using them very easily (better than the big toilet at home). - Julie

If you are lucky, the staff may do the lion's share of the toilet training for you. They are likely to have helped toilet train dozens of children before yours. A friend of mine had not trained her son by the time he was three as she had a particularly difficult second pregnancy. When she admitted this to the local kindergarten, one of the teachers got him toilet trained in a very short period of time.

Remember, you are just one person. If there is any time in your parenting life when it is okay to ask for help, then it is during potty training. Reach out to professional potty trainers; you may be pleasantly surprised with the outcome.

If You Suspect or Know That They Won't Be Helpful

Some childcare places do not have trained staff for toilet training or do not have the resources to deal with a child going through potty training. The first thing I suggest is to move your child to a place that does, if you can.

If that is not possible, then you need to think of some workarounds. No matter where your child is in the toilet training process, as long as he has some sort of clue, then be really positive about his progress to the staff. Talk them up. Say you still have an accident or two at home, but he is generally learning well. It is not lying so much as managing the teacher's expectations. This could backfire if your child has a bad accident day, but if that happens, show surprise and ask if there is anything more you can do so it can be better in the future. Remember your child needs to continue on his journey to be fully toilet trained despite any obstacles such as a reluctant childcare provider.

If the daycare insists on the child wearing diapers, but you don't want to confuse your child or take a step backwards in the training, you have two choices:

1. Conveniently forget to send her in diapers and send her in underwear, even if she is not completely toilet trained, OR
2. Put your child in training pants or pull-ups and tell her that this is only for daycare and at home she wears big kid underpants.

In both cases, encourage your child to go and pee independently or locate her favorite teacher and tug on his or her arm if she needs help to go.

The Good and the Bad

Whether the staff are on board or not, all childcare arrangements outside the home have one main positive and one main negative when it comes to toilet training. On the good side, many children respond well to the positive peer pressure of seeing other children going to the toilet. However, as daycare is so much fun, your child may not want to leave what he is playing with, and this can cause more accidents. In these cases encourage your child to tell a teacher to mind the toy or save his spot until he gets back.

ACTION ITEM – Approach your child care provider and get the lowdown on their policy and expertise around toilet training. Enlist their help if possible.

CHAPTER FIFTEEN

Out And About

Breathe That Fresh Air

Sooner or later you and your child need to actually leave the house. Now this is where it could turn into a disaster, but with some information, preparation and a strategy any issues can be easily dealt with.

You have a few decisions to make and things to consider, but you <u>can</u> leave the house and not get stressed. It is possible. Take a deep breath. Venture out your front door.

Mama Story – I took Nate to see 'Paddington' at the movies as a reward for pooping in the toilet. When we got there he was amazed to see all people at the cinema and asked, "Do they all poop in the toilet too?" - Sonia

The Number One Rule

Always, always, always encourage your little one to go to the toilet before you go out. If you are comfortable with the idea, go to the toilet yourself so he can watch you and see that it is a normal part of leaving the house. You may think you don't need to go, but you will.

Decide on Underpants or Training Pants/ Pull-ups

Will your child wear underpants out and about, or will you put her into training pants or pull-ups? You may not want to cause confusion by using pull-ups, but you can state that at home we wear underpants and when we go out we use pull-ups. For the sake of your blood pressure, this may be good for the initial few weeks. However, if you want to make diapers, including pull-ups, disappear forever, then a car seat protector pad or an old towel on the car seat is a must.

The Accident Bag

You thought you were done with that oversized diaper bag. But, for a while at least, you need to convert it to an 'accident' bag. Pack it and leave it in the car, or near the door so you can take it with you. Things to pack:

- hand sanitizer
- wipes or toilet tissues
- spare underpants (two or three)
- spare socks (this is one item easily forgotten)
- a full change of clothes such as trousers, shorts, dresses, stockings
- a spare pair of shoes or sandals (they can get quite wet during an accident)
- a couple of old towels
- a couple of spare plastic bags
- (optional) – a pull-up or two
- (optional) – foldable toilet seat insert

If you are in a hurry or want to pack lightly, then stuff a spare pair of toddler underpants, a small packet of wipes and a scrunched up plastic bag in your handbag or pocket. This minimalist kit helps in the case of one accident, but no more than that.

Know Where the Bathrooms Are or Bring a Travel Potty

Get yourself familiar with where the bathrooms are at your local hang outs – the supermarket, the mall, the library, your favorite café, local restaurants and the park. This often uses your detective powers again as some toilet locations are not that obvious.

Encourage your child to use big person toilets when you are out, even if they only sit on the potty at home. To assist, some parents bring a portable, foldable toilet insert for public toilets.

The alternative to this is to take a potty with you. There are special travel potties or you can bring a spare one from home in a plastic bag. This is especially good for longer car trips. If it is safe, you can pull over and use the potty. Many parents prefer not to bring potties into places they visit, but some do. Sooner or later, your little one will need to be able to do her business on an actual toilet.

Mama Story - I took the normal potty out in a plastic bag. Funniest moment was on about day five when out at a café, my son walked up to me, picked up the potty and started off for the bathroom with it on his head! He then had a pee in it and luckily didn't put back on his head. - Tania

Remind Your Child

When out and about, tell your child to let you know when he needs to go to the toilet. Also make sure your super sleuth skills are on high alert for that jiggle or look. You want to make sure he doesn't just run off, but that he also doesn't just stand there.

If There is An Accident

If you have an accident when you are out at the mall, a restaurant or the supermarket, try to clean up your toddler as much as you can and let a retail assistant, mall attendant or customer service person know. Even if you sponge up most of it, they will probably want to go and get a mop. Don't be *that* person and run off. These incidents happen every week and they have a procedure to deal with it.

At an appropriate point afterwards, talk to your toddler about the accident and come up with ways to avoid it in the future. Did she forget to tell you she needed to go, or did the urge come on too quickly? Her responses can help with planning future outings better.

Public Restrooms

There are two types of children when it comes to public restrooms. Some children love them; they always want to check them out and would happily spend all day in there. If you have a child like that, then rejoice. You can use any toilet anywhere.

However, public toilets can be quite intimidating for your little one. Toilets themselves can be scary (see the problems section for more), but public bathrooms have their own set of fear factors including:

- The sheer scale and size of the restrooms
- The number of grown ups going in and out of them

- Loud electric hand dryers, especially those new super fast ones (bring paper towels so you never have to use these)
- Auto-flushers which could go off at any time (if you are very organized, covering with a post-it note can often stop this)

If your child doesn't want to enter a public bathroom you may be able to entice him into the parent and child cubicle. If that doesn't work, then try to find a parent's room or disabled toilet that is separate from the main restroom. Or you may need to make sure you have a potty with you, in the car at least.

It is important to teach your child some basic etiquette for public bathrooms. She may not realize at first that she should not look under stalls, run off without you, flush repeatedly or splash water everywhere while washing hands.

The last issue is what to do if your opposite gender child wants to go into his or her own gender's restroom area. The general rule here is he or she should always stay with you. If you cannot convince your boy to come into the ladies, then find a separate disabled toilet or bring a travel potty with you.

At Other People's Homes

It may feel rude and a bit abrupt, but as soon as you turn up anywhere make it known to your host that your child is in the middle of potty training. Ask her where the toilet is (if you don't already know), and lead your toddler to it, so he is familiar with the lay of the land. Often, toddlers love checking out other people's bathrooms and toilets (even those that are scared of big public restrooms).

If you let your host know, then she won't be surprised that in the middle of a conversation, you turn away for a couple of seconds and say, "Let Mama know if you want to go pee". If it makes sense, encourage your child to play outside, as accidents outside on the lawn are not nearly as bad as inside on your host's favorite rug. Most people you visit will have an understanding of this trying time, and if there is an accident, she won't stop being your friend over it.

At the Park

Parks are the best places for a toddler who is toilet training. There is often a toilet block, but if there is an accident it will be outside on the ground and all you need to do is make sure you have an old towel or car seat protector mat for the ride home.

Some families encourage the ability to pee outside (standing up or squatting) if the urge overtakes the child. Other parents do not like to promote this option. It may be okay if there are no toilets around and you find a discreet bush to tuck behind. But if, like me, you look around to see your son standing in the middle of the garden feature of a popular picnic spot 'watering the forest,' then you should try to teach him the difference between peeing on the lemon tree at home and socially acceptable peeing while out and about.

Swimming

The best thing to do at a public pool is to check their policy. They may insist on special swim diapers until a certain age. To avoid any confusion, clarify to your child that the diapers are only for when they are swimming in the pool.

Car or Airplane Travel

Long car trips or airplane travel can be an especially trying time if you are in the middle of potty training. One suggestion is just don't go. If you still want or need to, the next best thing for your blood pressure is to put on training pants or pull-ups. If you want to avoid 'going back into diapers,' then make sure you have a couple of car seat protectors and old towels for accidents for car or airplane seats. Have lots of toilet breaks and insist your toddler at least try and see if there is any pee, even more than you would at home. Don't forget your accident bag with a change of clothes.

Now to Tackle the Night

You have all the strategies and tools in place to assist you during daytime toilet training, in and out of the home. But what about at night? Read on to find out.

ACTION ITEM – Put together an accident bag.

CHAPTER SIXTEEN
Nighttime

Night and Day

The approach to toilet training overnight is quite different from during the day. Whether you decide to split up day and night or want your child out of diapers all at once, read this before you start the nighttime part.

It is best not to even call it toilet training. The brain connections involved in being dry at night are mostly not part of conscious awareness. She needs to become aware of subtle physical signals. Don't mistake this to mean that you do not have to do anything – becoming dry at night still requires a devoted effort on your part. Don't shirk your parental responsibilities at this final hurdle!

Children become dry at night <u>only</u> when either:

- they have a big enough bladder to hold onto their pee overnight, OR
- they can wake up and empty their bladders (in the toilet) during the night.

This is often six months to a year after they are daytime trained. For example, if your toddler is daytime potty trained at two and a half, he may be over three before he is developmentally ready to be out of diapers at night.

Therefore it is important to note that this is not like the positive approach used during the day, possibly accompanied by incentives (see the next chapter). In fact, using external rewards could be detrimental to your child's understanding, as much of the outcome is beyond her conscious control. Be happy if there is nighttime success, but keep the sticker charts and chocolates away and tone down the praise. A simple 'well done' is usually sufficient.

One last thing – this book assumes that if you are looking to get your child out of diapers at night, then he has moved to a bed. Logistically, it is much harder to get to a toilet or potty from a crib, which means either you have to get up more or there is an increased likelihood of accidents. For the smoothest transition, move to a bed first and then start thinking about taking diapers off at night.

Should I Do it Now or Wait?

Like everything in this book, this is up to you and your child, and remember you can change your mind. The answers to these questions may help you to decide when to approach nighttime toilet 'training'.

- Does your child understand the feeling of needing to go to the toilet?
- Has he got the dexterity to get himself out of bed and to the toilet or potty by himself if need be?
- Do you think your child will learn better by doing it all at once or splitting it up?
- Do you think you will have less stress by doing it all at once or splitting the learning up?

- Does your child say she wants to go to bed without diapers?

Mama Story - I would have separated them because I heard that nighttime training comes later. But the first night when I went to put a diaper on my daughter she said, "No. Remember, no more diapers." She repeated my mantra and wouldn't let me put one on her. I let her do it (fearfully) but she was dry all night! And every night since. - Emma

The Main Sign Your Child May Be Ready

If your child is waking up dry at least a couple of mornings in a row, then this is the best indicator he could be ready. When he first gets out of bed in the morning check his diaper before you start your morning routine. If it is dry (or almost dry), then give diapers off at nighttime a go.

Mama Story - It was a good ten months after day training before Daisy was night trained. First they need to be able to make it through the night dry - apparently this is physiological so not something you can train. Then over summer she shared a room for three nights with another little girl who just wore a singlet and knickers to bed. Daisy made up her own mind that she wanted to be like her. - Marianne

Liquids Before Bedtime

A common question is about liquid intake before bedtime. You need a practical and realistic approach to this. For example, allowing water along with the evening meal is usually fine, but having a number of glasses after dinner may ruin the chances of a dry night. Some children are happy to remove the last milk in the bedtime routine and others will not give it up for dear life. It goes without saying that limiting the intake of bath water is a step in the right direction.

Monitor the situation – somewhere between dehydration and 14 trips to the toilet in the night is a good start. Note that if she is well hydrated during the earlier part of the day, then she will not want to drink as much in the evening.

Nighttime Without Diapers - The Process
Talk to your child and explain what is going on. Explain the plan including going to the toilet just before bed at night and as soon as he wakes in the morning. Note that accidents could happen and it is not a big deal. Check that he can get his pajamas down and up easily.

Set a bedtime routine, or keep to your usual one with the addition of going to the toilet just before bed. This is, without doubt, the most important part of the bedtime routine. You can even try to do this twice. For instance, just after bath-time, and then once again right before she hops into bed. If there is any place for rewards in nighttime training, then some parents use them to encourage that last toilet stop before bed. No one is judging you for it, do whatever works.

Now at this point you have two options. Both schools of thought are valid, and you may need to try both to see which works better for your child.

1. Leave your child for the rest of the night. This approach enables her brain signals to develop, but there is a chance

for more accidents. Her body will learn to 'hang on' or she will wake up by herself and take herself to the toilet or potty (or yell out for you to help her). Having a couple of nightlights – one in her room and one in the bathroom – can help this. An option here is to leave a potty in her bedroom, especially if she is a long way from the bathroom. However, you eventually want to encourage her to make it to a toilet, so this should be a temporary measure. OR -

2. When you go to bed, you can 'sleepwalk' or 'lift' him to the toilet for a 'dream pee'. This may hinder the correct brain signals developing, disrupt sleep and hinder his independence, BUT (and it's a big but) it can help prevent more accidents at night until his bladder learns to hold on better. To try and enhance brain connections, it's best that your little one is at least a bit awake, but sometimes this 'lifting' while practically asleep works really well.

It is worth repeating that whatever you decide, you can change your approach if it is not working. And know that your child will be dry at night eventually. For instance, helping her go to the toilet may just be a stopgap for a few weeks or months.

Mama Tip - One great tip for avoiding peeing in the bed at night is to put them on the toilet before the parent goes to bed. They are totally asleep and adorable but usually go when you place them in the position to go pee. It has saved us many nights of changing beds. At four years of age we are still putting her on the toilet before we go to bed. We are starting to notice that she is waking to go to the toilet but we are not fully there yet. I expect by the age of five she will be fully trained. Yah!
- Zoe

Accidents *May* Happen

Unlike the 'death and taxes' for daytime toilet training, you may never have nighttime accidents. Some families have found one child is always dry at night and another child has occasional or even frequent accidents. Having realistic (read LOW) expectations is a good place to start.

For the most part, if you are toilet training for nighttime, go from normal diapers to underpants. There are 'dry nite' diaper products (or pull-ups) that are like normal diapers but are not as absorbent. These seem to be a lot of money for an inferior product that just delays the inevitable of wearing actual underpants (under pajamas) at night. But for the sake of your precious sleep and blood pressure, and especially if you are going through a stage of many wet nights, then you could consider using these.

Regardless of whether you expect accidents to occur at night, and whether you are using a special nighttime diaper or underwear, a good investment is a mattress protector. There are two main types:

- a waterproof mattress protector that fits under the bottom sheet
- an absorbent bed pad with tuck in wings that fits over the bottom sheet

The over the sheet pads make changing the bed after an accident very easy - buy two so you can swap them out (search 'Brolly Sheets' on the internet). Perhaps use both types if the budget allows. At the very least, a couple of old towels can come in handy.

Nighttime Accidents – The Process

With nighttime accidents, you'll need your super powers again, as nothing tests your positivity, patience and calmness more than being woken from slumber and having to do a full change of bedding and clothing at 2am in the cold and dark… other than doing it again at 4am.

Remember no child wants to be wet and cold and he is certainly not doing it on purpose. Respond quickly, quietly and with as much gentleness as you can muster. Remove wet pajamas, clean up your tot and put him in something clean and dry. Take off wet bedding and replace. As noted above, this is where an over-the-top absorbable pad comes in very handy – often this is the only thing you need to swap out. Reassure your child that accidents sometimes happen and allow him to go back to sleep as soon as possible. If you run out of clean, dry sheets, a large towel can be used instead until morning.

Nighttime Accidents - When to Seek Help

Some children have no nighttime accidents, some have a spate of them and then stop, and some wet the bed once a week for months. Do not compare your child to any other, including her siblings. It can be years before a child is 100% dry at night. If you are really going through a bad patch, then you can consider putting your toddler back in diapers at night. After all, sleep trumps toilet training every time. But know that you need to dedicate some time to the overnight process again in the future.

Many children at five still wet their beds at night occasionally. A handful of children at seven or older still do, too. If your child is still wetting the bed and is school age, make sure she has a quick wash in the morning so there is no lingering smell. The last thing you need is to exacerbate the problem with teasing from classmates.

There is no 'normal' situation, and sometimes time is the best solution. But if you are concerned, seek professional or medical advice. There are some effective solutions to prolonged bed-wetting issues that can be tailored to the individual child. These include bladder training, bed-wetting alarms or prescribed medication that are all beyond the scope of this book.

ACTION ITEM – Decide on a plan to getting your little one dry at night.

CHAPTER SEVENTEEN
Incentives And Rewards

Do I Give My Child and Incentive or Reward During Toilet Training?

The easiest answer here is 'No'. However, the vast discrepancy between best practice (no reward) and what parents actually do (whole bags of M&Ms for one little pee) mean that there needs to be at least some discussion around this topic. The pros and cons of external motivators during toilet training could fill an entire book on their own, but here it is chunked down to the basics so you can make your own decisions.

Just so we are all on the same page, here are a couple of definitions:

- <u>Reward</u> – a benefit provided in recognition of achievement and given afterwards.
- <u>Incentive</u> – a benefit to motivate an individual to improve his behavior, promised beforehand.

The most important thing to take away from this chapter is that whichever way you do it, you need to find the 'something' that motivates your child to change or improve her behavior. If she doesn't care about the 'something,' then it won't be effective.

"But," you say, "I don't know what motivates my child." Or, "He is fairly good in most areas, but is it okay to reward him just for washing his hands, for instance? And what should I do if I want to stop giving him chocolate every time he goes?" Read on, but be prepared to be flexible.

A Reward In Itself

In theory at least, internal drivers are much more important than external rewards. There are three keys for keeping motivation high:

- knowing the purpose behind the task
- mastery of the task (a desire to improve)
- autonomy (control over the task)

If anything is a reward in itself, then learning to go to the toilet independently is it. It ticks the purpose, mastery and autonomy aspects in spades. This is all part of becoming a 'big kid,' which should be on repeat at your home. Sometimes these are not enough to drive behavior. So what are your other options?

Option One – Praise and Encouragement

Nothing beats good old-fashioned praise as a 'reward'. It's cheap, easy and always available. It helps to make going to the toilet not just a normal but an enjoyable experience for your little one. It should always be used before any other external incentive or reward, and in the short intense period, it should be the only motivator used.

Praise for trying and praise for succeeding, and try to be as specific as possible. Remember there are a lot of steps in the toileting process and he is bound to have done at least one part well.

Being encouraging can take many forms including smiles, hugs, high-fives, saying positive things, clapping your hands or doing a song and dance. See the "Stage One" chapter for more.

Option Two – The Sticker Chart

If praise does not cut it, or if you want to move rewards up a notch, then sticker charts can be a good form of encouragement. If you have not encountered sticker charts as a parent yet, potty training will get you knowing more about them than you ever thought possible. Sticker charts are easy to implement, inexpensive, and healthier than some other options. It's a good idea to give them a go before moving on to other incentives.

Get an old piece of paper and stick it to the wall inside or just outside of your bathroom. Keep it quite low down for little hands to be able to place stickers on it. Buy some stickers in advance and keep them out of sight (your toddler can choose a few packs when you do your initial shop for underpants and potties). Try not to think about how unhygienic that sticker chart will become as your – usually unwashed - toddler hands are putting stickers all over it.

It is up to you how you want to dish out the stickers. Does he get one each time he attempts to go pee or poo? Does she get one when she washes her hands? Does he get one when he tells you he needs to go? Usually at first, she gets one for any toilet training related task, however small. If you want to promote a particular thing as being important, then only give a sticker for that. For example, many children successfully empty their bladders well, but may need more encouragement to poo in the potty or toilet, so bringing out the stickers for that may help.

Sometimes, putting a sticker on the chart is enough of a reward. Alternatively, you can offer a sticker, and then after your tot has received say ten of them, you can give her a little present like a book or toy car. Your child must be old enough to appreciate this long-term milestone approach for it to work well.

Some children respond well to the sticker chart. Others do not. If your child pees, jumps up from the potty and before pulling up his pants is asking for a sticker, then you are onto a winner.

Mama Tip – We only used stickers, one for a pee, two for a poo. Then if you got enough you got a toy. - Raewyn

Option Three – Anything and Everything

The types of incentives and rewards you can use are only limited by your imagination. Remember the important thing is finding out what motivates the tiny human and using that. Here are some suggestions:

- Calling Grandma to tell her about pee in the potty.
- Getting a stone or marble after each toilet trip and putting it in a jar.
- Ringing a bell afterwards.
- Allowing some screentime (TV or computer game).
- Access to a special toy that is kept out of reach most of the time.
- A certificate of achievement (easy to make at home).
- A small gift of a toy, book, cool new underpants or a wrapped surprise.
- A special outing.

It's important to remain consistent, otherwise the connection between behavior and reward can be broken (you may want to break it later but we will get to that). So don't start something you cannot keep up due to budget or time constraints. As a side note, it's good to get your child used to rewards being only used at home, or at the very least, that she will get it back at the house if you are out and about.

Again, you can reward for each behavior you want to promote (marbles in a jar), or build up to a larger reward (a special outing). If something is not working, then change tack, but try to refrain from going bigger – go different.

Mama Story - When Adam first pooped on the toilet I took him to the store and let him choose about $50 worth of toys. He was thrilled, had gotten his reward and then seemed to not see the point in pooping in the toilet again for about a year. - Terri

Option Four – Sweets

No discussion of rewards would be complete without talking about rewarding with food, mostly of the sweet variety. Yes, candy, lollies, sweets, chocolate, lollipops, marshmallows, whatever you call it and whatever you choose, sweet food has been used as a reward by many a guilty, frazzled parent during toilet training.

This book is not going to stand in judgment over you, but please be aware of the potential power of sweets being used as a reward. You should not undertake this path lightly. Perhaps start with the smallest sweet food you can find – a mini-marshmallow or one jellybean for example.

Mama Story - I had a jar of jellybeans by the toilet for reward. Swore by it! Friend's kids who were at my house and went on the toilet got one too. Instant reward. - Paula

How to Stop the External Rewards

Eventually, you have to stop using stickers or chocolate, and Grandma is probably tired of the phone calls about pee in the potty. If you are lucky, the use of incentives will just fall away naturally over time. However, sometimes you need to intervene. Go down the list below and find an approach you think works best for your situation. Give it a good honest try.

1. Go cold turkey – simply remove the reward. Say it will not happen any more, or won't happen from X date, say two days from now (when the last lollipop is gone). No, you won't buy any more from the store. There is simply no more in the house to give.

2. Have a gradual withdrawal – for instance, get it down to one sticker for one part of the toileting process (washing hands) then fade it out altogether (if they don't ask for it, don't give them one).

3. Replace the sweet treat with sticker rewards or some other more neutral incentive. Stickers are not as exciting, so eventually your child should give them up on her own.

Daddy Story - We started with lollypops for poo. Sometimes she would poop five times in the day to get lollypops so we changed to stickers. - Harry

What is the worst that can happen with any of these? He may be upset and you may even get an extra accident or two, but it's very unlikely you will experience a full meltdown or regression. If you are committed to removing the reward, then stand your ground. You are the parent. You have made a responsible decision. Go back to basics and give him extra praise and encouragement for being a big boy and move on with your lives.

If you experience a severe negative reaction, then you are likely to be dealing with a behavioral issue rather than a toilet training problem. There is a difference between the two that is clearly explained in the next chapter.

Don't Overthink This

Rewards and incentives can make toilet training a lot more complex than it needs to be. Keep it simple. Start with praise, perhaps move on to a sticker chart, and only offer sweets if there is something you really want to incentivize. Know that you have the power to switch or stop at any time.

Two last things for when the toilet training is finished:

- Put the sticker chart away in your child's mementos box.
- Give yourself a reward or a treat for all your hard work.

ACTION ITEM – Think of what will motivate your child during potty training and stock up on it (stickers, chocolate or simply your cheery disposition).

CHAPTER EIGHTEEN

Problems And Solutions

Warning

Stop! Red light! Do not read this section of the book if you don't have to. It is the by far the longest chapter, but feel free to skip it entirely and get to the 'Busy Parent Summary' next.

If potty training your youngster is going swimmingly, then do not even glance in here. If you do, you will start worrying about things that you may never have to worry about.

The Good and the Bad News

Here is the bad news up front – if you encounter a particularly weird issue, it may not be covered here. This book covers solutions to the most common potty training problems. The good news is that instead of tailored solutions to every toileting problem under the sun, there is a formula for empowering you to figure out your own solution. Here is the formula:

Behavior – Reason – Solution

You observe your child's behavior (the easy part), work out the reason behind it (the hardest part) and then match up a solution to the reason (many suggested ones are in this book). Voila – problem solved! If you use this formula and you don't get your desired outcome, then hypothesize a new reason for the behavior and select another solution that fits that reason.

For instance, your child has resumed having frequent accidents. Is it because he doesn't like the new potty, is a bit scared of the toilet, got distracted or even did it on purpose? How you solve this issue relates to why it happened in the first place.

Main Reasons

Drilling down to why the behavior is happening is the key to solving your potty problems. Here are the main reasons behind toilet training issues:

- Doesn't get it - The child does not understand what is happening, hasn't learnt the process properly, or connections haven't been made.
- Doesn't care - The child understands but is easily distracted, doesn't seem to care and could even appear lazy.
- Fear/worry - The child has some anxiety, worry or fear around the transition or aspects of it (eg: the toilet itself).
- Low/Passive resistance - The child doesn't like or want the changes.
- High/Active resistance - The child is trying to engage in power struggles or control battles over the changes.
- Other - There is a medical issue or something else is going on.

Main Solutions

It's best to choose a solution that correlates with the behavior or reason. Here is a quick reference list of the main ones you could select:

- <u>Give it time</u> - Wait it out. Don't worry about it. Hope it comes right.
- <u>Reset</u> - Try again at a later date.
- <u>Pre-work</u> - Extra teaching and laying groundwork.
- <u>Normalize it</u> - Make going to the toilet part of the daily routine, including the occasional interruption to playtime.
- <u>Make it fun</u> – Make going to the toilet easy, exciting and enjoyable.
- <u>Consistency</u> - Emphasize your commitment and focus to toilet training.
- <u>Small steps</u> - Introduce some intermediate steps to allow change to unfold at a slower pace.
- <u>Physical needs</u> - Make sure your tot has enough water, nutritious food and quality sleep.
- <u>Security</u> - Offer reassurance and make him feel safe.
- <u>Praise</u> - Explain your expectations and follow up with encouragement.
- <u>Discipline</u> - Explain your expectations and follow up with consequences.
- <u>Control</u> - Give her more choices, independence or privacy.
- <u>Environment</u> - Change external aspects or circumstances.
- <u>Incentivize</u> - Utilize external rewards or incentives.
- <u>Medical</u> - Seek medical or professional advice.

When You Don't Know Where to Start

"This is all great in theory," you say, "but I have poop on my wallpaper! What do I do first?" Below are specific solutions to common problems, so check here first. You can also come back to the formula and lists above and work from there to get creative with your own solutions tailored to your child.

My Child Doesn't Want to Go And I Am Not Sure Why

At any stage in the toilet training process, if your child is reluctant to go on the potty or toilet and you are not sure why, then ask her. She may be able to tell you or communicate something to you. The first thing you must check is if anything is hurting or she is worried it will hurt. If there is a potential medical issue (like an urinary tract infection or severe constipation), then seek out appropriate help.

My Child Has No Idea What is Going On (Stage One)

After a week or so, if your tot really has no idea what is going on and can wet himself and just carry on with an activity like nothing has happened, then you may need to reassess whether now is a good time for potty training.

He may have shown a few signs of readiness, but for some reason the connections are just not there. He might still be too young (under two). He might have come down with a cold, or there are other distractions holding his attention (a new pet?). Ask yourself if there is anything you could have done differently (were you committed 100%)?

Your first option is to be really patient and offer more explanations and a whole heap of praise and encouragement. If you don't see much improvement in a few days, the best thing to do is just stop all your efforts and plan the short intense period again in a month or so. Put a diaper back on her and forget about it. Tell yourself it wasn't a complete failure, some learning MUST have gone in. At the very least, you had a lovely bonding time with your child.

Important – do not do this right in the middle of a big accident in a really dramatic way. Get to the end of the day, put a diaper on her for bedtime and then the next day continue to use diapers.

When you start again, look for signals from your child that he may be a bit more ready. Then try the short intense period first and go from there. Yes, it may be winter by then, but you can't have everything perfect. On a reset you may not even have to commit precisely to Stage One – just introduce the main parts that help develop brain-body connections.

My Child Has Some Idea But Potty Training is Not Going Well (Stage Two)

You are past the first couple of weeks and it is obvious that the brain connections are there. Your child has an understanding, but when she goes off to the toilet nothing happens. Or there may be frequent accidents (every day).

If she is trying, then she has obviously made some developmental progress but needs to fine-tune some of the basics. A reset is not usually advised. Remain committed and do not put her in diapers due to the accidents. Go back to some of the pre-work, explanations, modeling behavior and role-plays. Give her lots of praise and encouragement. Remain neutral about the accidents. This should right itself over time.

If there are accidents due to inattention, distraction, being engrossed with play or if it looks like he cannot be bothered moving to the potty, then the solutions above also work. In addition, you need more active day-to-day monitoring. Put breaks into his routine when he stops what he is doing and is told or is escorted to the toilet. Tell him that his toy will be there when he gets back. Even offer to bring it into the bathroom if it helps. Also be on the look out for the telltale jiggle and get him to the toilet. Do it lovingly and give him some wins of getting to the potty on time. Eventually he should realize that stopping for a minute to go to the toilet is much better than peeing his pants.

For both these cases, you could introduce an external incentive to improve the behavior, but these come with their own set of considerations (see the 'Rewards' chapter).

If she is an older child (over three years old) and it looks like she wants to learn but it's not happening well and there are a lot of accidents, then you may want to consider seeking medical advice.

My Child Has Accidents on Purpose (Stage Two or Three)

The first thing to note here is please be very clear about whether your child is deliberately having accidents or not. It can do more harm than good to accuse your child of having an accident on purpose when he did not. Give him the benefit of the doubt. Do not fall on the side of thinking your child is purposely creating accidents to ruin your life unless you have firm and irrefutable proof.

If she is busy with her toys and stands up and just goes, then she is not doing it on purpose, she just got her signals a little wrong. If he poops in a potty and then throws the potty across the room at you (yes, that is a true story), then you have a serious issue on your hands.

To sort out the immediate impact of having a non-accident accident, do not get mad, get scrubbing. Take your annoyance out on the sponge or mop and the floor. If your child is wet or dirty, sort him out first and then put him quietly in his room and tell him he is to stay there until you clean up the mess. If your child is older (say over three and a half), then get him to help clean up. The point is to inconvenience him while you are busy spending your time cleaning up the mess.

Afterwards, it may be necessary to consider whether this behavior is a reflection of a wider discipline issue with the child. See the next issue for solutions.

Mama Story - My son could make himself poo when he was really angry with me. It was a control thing rather than a toileting thing and I didn't really get that at the time. - Sally

My Child Is Showing Some or a Lot of Resistance (Stage Two or Three)

If your toddler starts demanding a diaper instead of underpants, refuses point blank to wash her hands, doesn't want to try to wipe her own bottom or you are having more tantrums than before, then you are probably looking at a general behavior issue and not a specific toileting problem.

Resistance can be looked at as a good thing – she is learning something new and is finding the change difficult or wants to stamp her own influence on the transition.

Decide if you want to intervene and directly sort out the behavior or if you think it will sort itself out on its own (be honest here). That is, do you want to spend time and energy resolving it? It is not recommended to have a complete reset at this point unless nothing else works.

If you do need to fix the problem (throwing poo-filled potties comes under this category), then you have some options. Does your tiny human need more routine and structure or more love and empathy (or both)? Does he simply need more sleep or nutritious food to calm his behavior? Look at your parenting and decide how to gain back the respect and responsible behavior you deserve in your family.

For tantrums, address them as you normally would. Remove your reaction to them. This may have the added disadvantage of the child wetting his pants, but so be it. Having a 'natural' consequence like this may actually encourage the child to behave better.

One way to assist a change is to bring in a consequence to behaving badly. A consequence is small and immediate, for example, taking a toy away for the day or not being allowed to watch her favorite TV show.

Another way, which at first may seem like it would provide an outcome contrary to what you want, is to give your child more independence. By providing privacy (allowing the toilet door to be shut) and giving her choices (which pair of underpants to wear for example), she will feel more in control and therefore embrace the transition better.

My Child Goes Pees Just Fine but Will Not Poo in the Toilet or Potty (Stage Two)

So your toddler trundles off to the potty and happily pees, but when it comes to number twos he instead goes behind the sofa and poops in his underpants. Or he waits for the bedtime diaper to be put on him and then five minutes later there is a poo 'present' for you. Or perhaps he gets really irritated and acts up a lot and you notice that there hasn't been a bowel movement for a couple of days or more.

Not wanting to poop in the toilet or potty is a very common problem, especially for boys. No one is quite sure why. Usually it is not anything to do with being able to physically detect pee better than poo. In general, bowel control actually occurs before bladder control.

The best theory is that the child does not feel safe pooping into a toilet bowl or out in the open into a potty. Somehow the diaper makes her feel more secure. It is even hypothesized that kids want to hold onto their poo. They are possessive about them and reluctant to give them up.

Whatever the reason, you need to address this fast and effectively. You do not want to repeat the situation of a four-year-old we knew, who months after being successfully toilet trained for pee, would take off his underwear, go and get a diaper, put it on himself and poop in it. You can of course just get rid of all the diapers, but you may still need them for nighttime. And eliminating diapers does not actually mean your young one will poop in the proper place – you may just end up with worse accidents to clean up.

The first thing to do is make sure it is not an environment problem – that he is scared of the toilet or is finding his new potty uncomfortable. Usually you will know this up front as peeing will be an issue as well. If he is fearful, see that section later in this chapter.

Second, make sure that your child has a balanced diet with lots of water, plenty of vegetables and a good dose of high-fiber food. Especially if your tot is not pooping at all for a period of time, she cannot stay constipated forever. If you know her diet is good, at the very least you can rule out a purely physical problem.

The third solution is to revisit the basic potty training strategies. Recharge your commitment. Get really good at super-sleuthing when a bowel movement is imminent (eg: red face, looking strained), and encourage your toddler to sit on the toilet or potty (even if the poo is 'hiding'). Explain what is required again and give lots of praise and encouragement for trying, even if nothing happens.

Mama Story - I took a trip to see my parents. I went for a nap and while I was asleep Nate asked for a diaper to poop. My Dad refused to get him one. Dad put him on the toilet and he eventually went. "Yay Poppy" I was so happy when I found out. The next time he asked for a diaper I refused and put him on the toilet. It took 90 minutes of waiting but he went. It got better each time until in about four days he was happy to use the toilet. - Sonia

The next solution is to add an external incentive. Perhaps reinstate the sticker chart just for number twos (maybe with some new cool stickers).

Mama Story - Well after he was toilet trained successfully for pee, we were still getting accidents for number twos. After a while we decided we needed to up the ante. We went to the store and Dylan got to choose a small monster truck toy. However, the toy remained in the packet and he wasn't allowed to open it until he had done his first poo in the potty. Yes, we felt we were being mean, what parents wouldn't? Eventually (after a few days), a poo was squeezed out into the potty and the monster truck packet was opened. Once he had done it once, bowel movements in the potty occurred regularly. He just needed the first 'win' to get it. He often shows the monster truck to visitors and tells them that he got it for pooping in the potty. - Julie

If this doesn't work, or it doesn't sit well with you, then another way to promote going poo in the toilet is let your child still poops in his diaper but when he looks like he is about to, insist he is in the bathroom or toilet area where he should be pooping. It seems counter-intuitive and like it wouldn't work, but introducing these intermediate steps allows the child to learn at his pace. Sooner or later your child associates poo with the proper area (toilet or potty) and starts to do them there.

Mama Story - Adam wouldn't poop on the toilet after his one initial time. I tried everything to encourage him on but nothing worked. I finally got some advice to let Adam poop in his diaper but to do it in the toilet room. He got over his aversion in only a few days and then he was on the toilet to poop, no worries. - Terri

My Child is Holding On Too Much (Stage Two)

Congratulations are in order as your gorgeous girl has garnered her brain development to such a degree that she not only recognizes the signals to empty her bladder, but has learned that she can hold on as well. That takes some control. However, it is not something to be taken lightly as it could cause a medical problem such as a urinary tract infection (UTI) if it is not addressed.

The main thing to observe is whether this occurs in a specific situation or is a general problem. Some children do not like going at the daycare center, and hold on all day, only to have an accident in the car on the way home. If it is a specific situation such as this, then it is best to go back to square one, lots of encouragement and praise for going to the toilet at the daycare. Work with the teachers and see if you can provide the most secure environment so your child feels safe going pee there. Maybe he needs an adult (you) to be with him in the bathroom area for a couple of days. Give these options a try.

If this is a general problem, then use your detective skills to look for the jiggling movements or pained expression and then escort her to the toilet. Sometimes all it takes is a gentle reminder, "I think you need to go toilet now." If this doesn't work, then take her into the bathroom and run the water in the sink or put the shower on and see how long she lasts with a full bladder listening to running water. See how long you last!

My Child Loves the Toilet a Bit Too Much (Stage One or Two)

This is perhaps a problem that other parents would love to have, but it can be a real issue for some families. It can present itself in a number of ways. Your tot loves to pull toilet paper off the roll and run around the house with it. He enjoys flushing the toilet repeatedly. She wants to sit on the potty for hours, even getting a book to read or a toy to play with while she is doing her business. Or he loves washing his hands so much that he fills up the sink, gets soap everywhere and generally has a lot of fun soaking his sleeves.

If this behavior lasts a day or two it is just your curious young child expressing his understanding of the toileting process. If you don't mind a bit of wasted paper or splashed water, then leave it alone and the behavior will right itself in a couple of days.

Note that if this curiosity extends to playing with poo, making poo wall art drawings or throwing it around, then of course this needs to be addressed immediately. Even very young children can learn quickly what is not appropriate behavior.

If you want to change any of the behavior, then it is back to basic parenting 101 – explaining what is expected and praising better outcomes. She may not even know how much toilet paper to use – show her. Introduce a discipline procedure for less desired behaviors such as a small consequence of taking one of his favorite toys away for the day. You could offer rewards, but you may be making further problems for yourself (see 'Rewards' chapter).

Mama Tip - Make sure your toothbrushes are kept out of reach of little hands and the sink, otherwise you will find that they will get washed along with everything else. - Bianca

My Child Got It and Now Has Lost It (Stage Three)

The issue of regression is unfortunately a common one. You have toilet trained your child and then – BOOM – she starts having accidents, wants her diaper back on or hardly ever makes it to the bathroom on time. Sometimes this is just a wobble in the road and after a couple of days of cleaning up accidents, it rights itself with no input from you.

If it continues, then you need to find out if there is a specific reason behind the regression. Many times it is due to there being a new baby in the family. Maybe the child is missing one-on-one attention (or any attention), or maybe she wants to be more like the baby and wear diapers. Regardless of exactly why a new baby disrupts toilet training, one thing that helps is to tell her she is a big sister now. Get her to help you with the baby and remind her that only babies need diapers. This approach has the combined effect of giving her attention and reminding her she is the big kid who can use the toilet.

Regression may happen due to other changes or disruptions – from moving to a different bedroom, moving house, a parent changing jobs or going back to work, to a change of childcare provider. It may be something minor that has caused it, for instance, an accident that was perceived as a bit embarrassing. There may be no external incident, or none that you know about. If at all possible, go back one step from where the issue originates and refocus your efforts and training from that point. Maybe she only has an accident around dinnertime, when she is tired. If so, even if she can take herself off to the bathroom during the rest of the day, introduce a toilet break at that time and escort her there yourself.

You have done some hard yards to get to this point, you know your child has the developmental and physical ability to be fully toilet trained, so he just needs to be reminded, with lots of love and support, how important it is.

Lastly, if there is some serious trauma like a death in the family that leads to regression, then you may need to ask for additional medical or professional help.

My Child is Scared of or Dislikes the Toilet (Stage Three)
It is a very common problem to have a toddler who does not want to do his business on the toilet, as he is a bit afraid of it. The first thing that needs to be determined is exactly what he dislikes or what is scary. It could be any or all of the following:

- Is the toilet room dark?
- Is the toilet seat cold?
- Is the toilet too big and he finds it hard to climb up?
- Does the toilet seat seem too wide and is he worried about falling into the toilet?
- Does he not like the sound of the flush?
- Are poops splashing into the toilet a worry for him?
- Does he not like how the contents in the toilet just disappear after a flush?

Mama Tip - I wouldn't have let him watch movies like 'Flushed Away' or 'Monsters Inc' - I don't think they helped! - Lola

I bet you had no idea of the number of things that could be a worry for your child. The exact solution relates to the main reason for his fear.

Make the toilet as comfortable, easy to use and inviting as possible. Have an insert and a footstool handy. Let him play with his favorite toy in there. A practical thing to do for the poo-splashing issue is to put some toilet paper in the toilet first to stop the splash back. Tell your child you won't flush the toilet until he has left the area. These small practical measures do help.

Then add other general solutions as required. Refocus your commitment to the toilet, remind him that he is a big boy and re-emphasize how normal it is to go to the toilet. Let him watch you go. Also, you can up the fun factor by giving him lots of encouragement or introducing external rewards (you have been warned about the downsides of this).

My Child is Doing a Bedtime Stall Tactic (Stage Two or Three)

Your little one is daytime trained but still in diapers overnight. She is in bed and then you hear her say, "I need to go potty." What do you do? You want to encourage her to go on the potty when she senses the need to go, but it's bedtime and she needs to go to sleep. Your child absolutely loves this as not only does it extend bedtime, but it definitely gets your attention and puts you at her beck and call.

Make sure you tell her to try and go just before the diaper goes on at night. At the very least this sets her up for a good nighttime routine when she is not in diapers anymore overnight.

Then there are a few tactics you can try. Sometimes just waiting it out is enough and your child stops doing this after a week or two.

If this doesn't work, then give her one or two chances to go to the toilet and then cut it off. Tell her you will not be taking her to the toilet again. Give her a choice of going in her diaper, taking herself off to the toilet, or perhaps put a potty in her bedroom and telling her to use that. For the second two options, you will probably have to help her, but she doesn't need to know that.

If you know that this nighttime sleep avoidance strategy is likely to occur, then pull your tot's bedtime forward a bit. This is a variant on the 'consequence' discussed above and also has the added bonus of allowing her to still go to sleep at a reasonable time.

My Child Has Slightly Wet or Soiled Underpants (Stage Three)

Your little one is fully toilet trained in the daytime but you notice that there are some dribbles in his pants. This is very common. The positive is that he has a lot of control to stop any further peeing. Or you see a bit of soiling in his underwear. Usually both these issues resolve over time, but if you want to give him a bit more attention, then ask your child to change his own underwear if it becomes dirty. For soiling, re-teach the wiping technique.

Mama Story - For a long time afterwards, maybe six months, he would start to go and do two to three drops in his undies before holding it in and running to the toilet. I wondered if he was ever going to recognize the feeling of needing to go? But he did, one day it just clicked. - Libby

My Child Has A Specific Problem Not Covered Here

These are the main problems that come up time and time again, but of course there are a myriad more. Remember that whatever behavior is displayed try to search out a reason for it and get creative on a solution that best matches the reason.

Always remember, there are no new problems when it comes to toilet training. Someone somewhere has encountered what you are going through, so ask for or search out help if you are really struggling.

You have made it to the end of an entire book on potty training. Can you believe it? I really hope you didn't read this chapter unless you needed to, but nevertheless, you are basically finished. The next few pages contain a handy quick reference summary and some final thoughts on toilet training, parenting and life.

CHAPTER NINETEEN
Busy Parent Summary

Busy Parent DECISIONS
Decide on these aspects of toilet training:

- Names for 'toilet talk' in your family.
- Use of a potty, the toilet or both.
- Whether your child will go commando, use underpants, training pants, pull-ups or a combination of these options.
- Will your initial focus be on daytime training at first or will you incorporate nighttime at the same time?
- Are external rewards such as stickers, sweets or toys going to be part of potty training?

Busy Parent ACTIONS
Follow these action steps for a smooth toilet training transition:

- Observe whether your toddler is displaying some of the signs of readiness to start potty training.
- Choose a date to start potty training when there is little distraction and you are ready to dedicate your focussed attention to it.
- Create some goals including 'out of daytime diapers by x time or in x amount of time'.

- Lay some groundwork by doing tasks that show going to the toilet as normal including talking about going to the toilet, reading books about it, showing her the process and explaining the intention to start toilet training soon.
- Talk to significant others in your life and tell them you will be potty training your child soon. This includes your partner, other children in the family, grandparents and teachers at the childcare center or kindergarten. Enlist their help if appropriate.
- Go shopping for toilet training items (see list below).
- Do Stage One - The Short Intense Period of toilet training for a few days.
- If Stage One works well move onto Stage Two – Active Maintenance.
- During Stage Two start daytime naps without a diaper and encourage more independence.
- Move on to Stage Three and start using the toilet exclusively (store the potty away).
- Work out a plan to getting your little one dry at nighttime (during or after Stages One to Three).

Busy Parent SHOPPING List

- About 20 or 30 pairs of kids underpants (with a picture on the front)
- Optional - 'branded' underpants (for example with a favorite Disney character on the front)
- Optional - training pants (washable) or pull-ups (disposable)
- Potty or potties
- A new toilet seat or toilet seat insert

- A small footstool or step
- Anti-bacterial hand soap
- Toilet paper and perhaps flushable bottom wipes
- Cleaning supplies for accidents such as rubber gloves, paper towels, cleaning wipes, cloths or sponges, a mop, a bucket, disinfectant, carpet cleaner, detergent and stain remover
- A little notebook to record those gems that your toddler will say during this time
- Optional - stickers, sweets or small toys for rewards
- Waterproof mattress protectors or absorbable bed pads

Busy Parent ACCIDENT Strategy

Your strategy may differ between a pee or poop accident but basically:

- If possible take your child and sit her on the potty/toilet to remind her of what she should do.
- Remove soiled clothes from your child.
- Clean up your child.
- Clean up yourself, if necessary.
- Clean up the floor and any other area involved.

Busy Parent SOLUTIONS Guide

Use the 'Behavior-Reason-Solution' formula to determine the best solution to problems you encounter during potty training. That is:

1. Observe your child's behavior.
2. Work out the reason behind it.

3. Match up a solution to the reason to try and solve the problem.

Here are the main reasons behind toilet training issues:

- Doesn't get it
- Doesn't seem to care
- Fear or worry
- A low or high resistance to change
- Other such as a medical issue

Here are some main solutions:

- Give it time / wait it out
- Reset and start again later
- Do extra pre-work
- Normalize going to the toilet
- Make going to the toilet seem fun
- Re-emphasize your commitment and focus to toilet training
- Small or intermediate steps
- Check all her physical needs are adequately taken care of
- Offer reassurance and make him feel safe
- Praise and encouragement
- Discipline and consequences
- Give her more control, choices, independence or privacy
- Change the external environment or circumstances
- Use external rewards or incentives
- Seek medical or professional advice

CHAPTER TWENTY
Final Thoughts

This book is about potty training your child, but deep down it is about you.

When you take your toddler through this challenging transition, I have no doubt that you will discover even more about yourself as a parent, teacher and human being.

Will you stay committed and keep to task? Will you be calm and positive most of the time? Would you enjoy doing a happy dance after the 17th pee-pee in the potty, or would you feel ridiculous? How well will you hone your super-sleuth powers over time? Could you repeat yourself over and over without going bat-crazy?

As mentioned at the start of the book, potty training is not something outside of normal parenting that needs to be over and done with. It is actually an integral part of your child's development and a significant milestone on the ladder of independence that you will coach him to achieve.

Please remember that no matter how this transition goes, you are a wonderful parent and amazing person.

Lift your head out of this book, take a deep breath and smile. Now, go and find the tiny human and give her an enormous hug.

Overload him with smoochy kisses. Tell that beautiful child of yours that you love her to the moon and back and always will.

Acknowledgments

Without a doubt I would not have written this book without the amazing support and accountability provided by the SPS community, especially from Stephanie and Marcy. Shout out to Chandler and the team too!

I have massive appreciation for the busy parents who completed the potty training survey. Thank you for taking your time to supply your sometimes horrifying, sometimes hilarious and always straight-up honest answers to the survey questions.

To Andrew and our two beautiful tiny humans, Dylan and Eloise. I live in a perpetual state of astonishment about how fortunate my life is.
Thank you for making me laugh every single day.

About The Author

Julie had aspirations of being a writer since she was very young but somehow got sidetracked into the corporate world. After the birth of her first child, Dylan, she rediscovered her creative side with a popular blog about her ride on the parenting rollercoaster at cherishmama.com.

'Easy Peasy Potty Training' is the first in a series of 'how to' books for busy parents. The aim of the books is to provide simple and straightforward information on parenting topics. By reading the books, parents can avoid all the time taken up searching for often confusing and conflicting advice. Instead, parents can spend time with the beautiful tiny humans in their life and do what makes their hearts sing.

Julie lives with her family in a small, magnificent country at the bottom of the world where you may find her trying to bake the perfect chocolate brownie.

DOWNLOAD THE BUSY PARENT SUMMARY

For all you wonderful, busy parents, I have created a summary sheet of the main actions to take and shopping items to buy for toilet training.

Head to cherishmama.com and get hold of your copy today.

Easy Peasy Potty Training

The Busy Parents' Guide to Toilet Training with Less Stress and Less Mess

Julie Schooler

THANK YOU FOR READING THIS BOOK

Thanks for choosing this book to assist you in
toilet training your tiny human.

Please leave a helpful and honest review on Amazon so that it can
help other busy parents when they decide to potty train their child.

Click into Amazon.com to leave a review today.

35982549R00083

Made in the USA
Middletown, DE
20 October 2016